Pastor Phil Hotsenpiller has writte
It is an eloquent cry from a Christian leader's heart and conscience as he watches his beloved America—the greatest
experiment in freedom and decency in history—approach
midnight. If all, or even if only a majority, of religious (not
just Christian) leaders had the courage of Pastor Hotsenpiller,
it would not be "Midnight in America." But as we saw during
the COVID lockdowns, the great majority of churches and
synagogues not only obeyed secular authority but also obeyed
irrational secular authority.

This book is addressed to Christians, but you don't have
to be a Christian to take the central message of *It's Midnight
in America* seriously: America has lost its way because Americans have abandoned the Bible, the basis of American and
Western civilization. When you abandon the base, everything
built upon it crumbles, and you lose everything.

If you are a Christian, it is urgent that you give a copy to
your pastor, because if America's Christians lose their way,
there is no hope for America. And I say that as a religious Jew.

—Dennis Prager, Co-Founder of PragerU;
Nationally Syndicated Radio Talk Show Host

Two biblical readings have strengthened me throughout my
life. Both have come into far more meaning in recent years:
Psalm 23 and Isaiah 6:8. America now stands in the valley of
the shadow of death, and unless each of us decides to stand up
and speak out against the evil forces we face, our nation risks
perilous times. In his seminal read, *It's Midnight In America*,
Phil Hotsenpiller outlines why, what's next, and how to arise
from the dark times facing America by rediscovering our biblical values and principles. Phil teaches us, once again, to be
fearless in the eyes of God and to never give up as people of
faith.

—Lt. General Michael T. Flynn, US Army

America is in a moment of *crisis*. I have traveled across hundreds of cities in the last three years and witnessed this firsthand while also experiencing the power of God moving mightily amid the brokenness. Now more than ever we need leaders, writers, and pastors who "know the times and the seasons" in which we live. Phil is one of those. May this book be a beacon of light and hope in the midst of a dark season.

—Sean Feucht, Let Us Worship

Pastor Phil Hotsenpiller is one of America's most prophetic pastors and is at the forefront of most influential pastors in the world today. His new book, *It's Midnight in America*, pulls back the veil on what the devil is doing, what God is doing, and what the righteous on earth need to do to see America and the world saved. Pastor Hotsenpiller is a prolific author, speaker, innovator, and communicator who draws from decades of innovative leadership and spiritual insight to bring a timely word to the body of Christ. I could not recommend this book more highly.

—Pastor Jürgen Matthesius, Awaken Church

Phil Hotsenpiller is creating a hope narrative in what might be America's darkest hour, but he isn't doing it by coddling us. He presents a prophetic perspective on correcting our course and getting back on track. Phil and his wife pastor in one of the hardest regions in the world, Southern California, with an uncompromised faith and conservative values, and they are on the front lines of the cultural war. I am so glad he is speaking into this with his unique perspective as a business leader turned pastor. He is a father, grandfather, and spiritual father, and you will feel that come through as your perceptions of what is happening are formed by a biblical worldview that will give you unshakable hope amid intense pressure that you are probably already feeling. This is a now book!

—Shawn Bolz, The Shawn Bolz Show

Phil Hotsenpiller has once again blessed us with a superbly written book regarding the prophetic warnings to our faith and nation. He balances the rich history and encouragement of biblical Scripture to inspire us to "put on the full armor of God." *It's Midnight in America* is a call to action to become the "physical and spiritual strength" within our neighborhoods and the "blacksmiths" who forge the swords for this spiritual battle. This book is inspired by acknowledging God's divine protection and the story we're still living through.

—Retired Colonel Michael Chené, USMC

In our nation's darkest hour, it is time for godly leaders to raise a standard and take an unapologetic stand for truth. My friend Phil Hotsenpiller is doing precisely that, not only with this book but in countless ways besides. In an era of moral cowardice and timidity, God's people are being offered an infusion of courage to rise to the occasion. Be emboldened by the voice of an overcomer so that you too can grab ahold of God's promises with unwavering faith.

—Dr. Ché Ahn, Harvest Rock Church, Pasadena, CA

Phil Hotsenpiller, a steadfast leader and pastor, navigated one of America's most challenging times and years in 2020, notably in California, holding firm to his faith in Christ and the call on their community. In his book *It's Midnight in America*, he illuminates our current times while inspiring readers not to lose sight of the call of God on their lives.

—Brian Barcelona, Founder/President of One Voice

It's Midnight in America by Phil Hotsenpiller is cold water in the face of the comatose church. It reveals with brilliant clarity the threats facing America, explaining step by step how the enemies of our liberties noiselessly encroached on our freedoms while we slept. But most importantly, Phil gives hope by laying out the courageous path we must take to be delivered from this precipitous place. *It's Midnight in America* is captivating, brilliant, fast-paced, and destined to be a Christian classic. I highly recommend that every freedom-loving American read it ASAP!

—WILLIAM J. FEDERER, NATIONALLY KNOWN SPEAKER AND BEST-SELLING AUTHOR

Americans are uneasy as our nation is careening toward the end of history. In his new book, Phil Hotsenpiller weaves ancient prophecies and current headlines to help bring a sense of order to the madness. He explains our fear and shows how we can all find peace in this unsettling time. The Bible is a self-authenticating book; it displays its authority by presenting the events of history ahead of time. *It's Midnight in America* shows us how to read these ancient prophecies and understand our present times.

—FLOYD BROWN, FOUNDER, THE WESTERN JOURNAL

Phil Hotsenpiller is a bold American pastor who believes that God gives rights and that governments are created to uphold those rights. The governments of the earth, the World Economic Forum, and secular thought leaders are rapidly pushing for the people of the planet to embrace the globalist agenda. Pastor Hotsenpiller has only become more resolved in his commitment to reawaken America to the biblical values and principles that made America great. He will not conform to the globalist mindset; instead, he chooses to do what is good and acceptable and the perfect will of God. I endorse Pastor Phil Hotsenpiller and know this book will bless you.

—CLAY CLARK, FOUNDER AND PRESIDENT, THRIVE 15

It's Midnight in America shines the light of truth in what appears to be one of America's darkest hours. Pastor Phil Hotsenpiller, with his vast biblical and historical knowledge, knits these crucial pieces together while maintaining the foundation of the Word of God. His book is a call to action for the church in a historic hour where we are meant to carry forth the standard that almighty God is raising. The kingdom of darkness attempts an advance to alter the sacred order from God, which is moving from darkness to light. The church in this hour needs to be the voice crying out in the wilderness, "Prepare ye the way of the Lord," and through the authority we have in Christ Jesus operate in the power we are meant to.

It's Midnight in America helps to equip believers and educate those seeking truth in an atmosphere of deception and lies. We must learn from the cycles of history the enemy operates in and draw very close to the Lord to receive the strategies from heaven to be victorious in an hour where much is at stake. This book calls for pastors to be shepherds in an hour of showmen, and Pastor Phil, through this book, does just that: stands as a shepherd among wolves.

—AMANDA GRACE, ARK OF GRACE MINISTRIES

Are you open to an experience that will stretch your intellect, challenge your anxiety, fuel your boldness, and provide a solid solution for the direction of your life? I am excited to report that I could not stop reading this book until the last page. It is a must-read for all who seek purpose and meaning for life's journey now and forever. It's time to set priorities in our lives and the lives of our families, organizations, and nation. It is approaching midnight in America, and the future won't wait. I enthusiastically recommend *It's Midnight in America*.

—GEORGE L. HAINES, PhD, JD; PRESIDENT, WORLDWIDE FINANCIAL CONSULTANTS

God gave Pastor Phil Hotsenpiller many gifts, not the least of which is the gift of prophecy. In this prophetic work, Pastor Phil is the watchman on the wall, sounding the alarm. His newest book is a road map for all of us to ensure that we are found on the right side of God when the hour of midnight strikes.

—JAMES ROGAN, FORMER MEMBER OF CONGRESS

It's Midnight in America is a true biblical masterpiece unraveling the prophetic signs and symbolism of the times we find ourselves in. Are you ready for what's coming? Pastor Phil provides an insightful revelation road map for believers, intertwining Scripture with current events and delivering a glimpse of what the future holds. Buckle up!

—Pastor Dave Scarlett, Founder/President, His Glory

I've had the honor of working with Phil Hotsenpiller for nearly ten years, and in that time I have come to appreciate his wisdom and insight. His historical and biblical knowledge is vast, and I have learned much. His book *It's Midnight in America* is a timely and needed message, speaking to our current era and encouraging us to meet the moment.

—Kim Walker-Smith, Award-winning Musical Artist

This book clearly addresses the shocking trends and events of our day with biblical prophecy. With all the seismic changes taking place domestically and globally, *It's Midnight in America* is a valuable reference for understanding the latest challenges and how we can be exceedingly victorious in their midst.

—Brad Dacus, President, Pacific Justice Institute

I had the pleasure of co-hosting a television series with Pastor Phil Hotsenpiller called *Friends of Israel* with evangelicals. I was amazed at Phil's knowledge and love for Israel, the Bible, and the Jewish people. His insight and understanding of the Holy Land is very inspiring. I consider him a righteous man, a friend, a wonderful teacher, and a gifted writer.

—Steven Paul, Producer/Filmmaker

We live in prophetic times: perilous, perplexing, and—for followers of Jesus—exciting as we witness God's ancient promises fulfilled before our eyes in real time. Yet, as Phil Hotsenpiller reminds us in his powerful and timely new book, Christians must also remember that as we eagerly anticipate our Savior's glorious return, He never said these days would be easy—especially for His church.

As the world grows increasingly dark and America strays dangerously further from its Judeo-Christian foundations, God is looking for a few good men and women to step up and fulfill the biblical mandate to be salt and light. *It's Midnight in America* provides a blueprint to do that and shows why the days ahead are not cause for fear but a renewed and empowered faith.

—ERICK STAKELBECK, HOST, *THE WATCHMAN WITH ERICK STAKELBECK*

America and the world are bearing witness to the disturbing signs of these times—from apostasy and crime in increasingly unimaginable ways to the abandonment of our moral compass and acceptance of child sacrifice, all in the name of our selfish desires. We are becoming like the godless societies before us who chose death and not life. Phil Hotsenpiller's new book, *It's Midnight in America*, will shock you into a righteous response as you realize that we are running out of time.

—BILL MARTINEZ, NATIONALLY SYNDICATED RADIO HOST

IT'S MIDNIGHT IN AMERICA

PHIL HOTSENPILLER

CHARISMA
HOUSE

IT'S MIDNIGHT IN AMERICA by Phil Hotsenpiller
Published by Charisma House, an imprint of Charisma Media
1150 Greenwood Blvd., Lake Mary, Florida 32746

Cover design by Michael Barkulis

For more resources like this, visit charismahouse.com and the author's website at InfluenceChurch.org.

Cataloging-in-Publication Data is on file with the Library of Congress.
International Standard Book Number: 978-1-63641-360-0
E-book ISBN: 978-1-63641-361-7

1 2024
Printed in the United States of America

Most Charisma Media products are available at special quantity discounts for bulk purchase for sales promotions, premiums, fund-raising, and educational needs. For details, call us at (407) 333-0600 or visit our website at www.charismamedia.com.

Portions of this book were developed using ChatGPT.

I dedicate this book to Tammy, my wife, friend, mother of our children, and colleague in ministry. Your devotion to God and His kingdom is a daily inspiration to me. I love you and look forward to all that God has planned for us in the future.

Contents

Introduction

I<small>T'S MIDNIGHT IN</small> America!

The church is asleep and slumbering in the night. Like Samson, we haven't realized that the power has departed, and like those who sleep, we are unaware of what is happening around us. We cling to our comfort like a child holding a toy.

It's midnight in America!

The spirit of fear has paralyzed us into believing the ancient lie that appeasement is better than courage and conformity is preferable to freedom. The church is so hungry to be accepted by the world that it has relinquished its power, forfeited its birthright, and accepted its place as nonessential.

It's midnight in America!

Lost in a maze of appeasement, the church expects little from God. Gone are the Elijahs of old who called down the power of God. Gone are the days of bold prophets who spoke out against the sins of a nation. Is it any wonder why we don't see more signs, wonders, and miracles?

It's midnight in America!

We are on the doorstep of the return of Christ. Every day we see more and more signs of His return. But are we ready?

Unraveling Midnight: A Journey Through Prophecy

In the Bible, certain words and symbols hold profound significance, transcending time and speaking to the hearts of humanity across generations. *Midnight* is one such word that carries multi-faceted meanings. It symbolizes deliverance, miracles, judgment, and unexpected events. This book seeks to explore the depths of these meanings, offering readers a wakeup call—a call to action in the context of our lives in America today.

At its core, this book is an exploration of end-times prophecy, providing readers with a sense of urgency given the times we find ourselves in. As we witness the ever-accelerating pace of global events and uncertainties, the word *midnight* becomes a poignant reminder of the need to be prepared for what lies ahead. By delving into biblical prophecies and connecting them with current events, readers are empowered to discern the signs of the times they live in.

We will uncover diverse shades of meaning that *midnight* conveys. From tales of miraculous deliverance to stories of divine judgment, this word signifies a contrasting tapestry of hope and warning. It calls us to embrace hope in the face of fear, acknowledging that even in the darkest of hours, faith can lead to unshakable strength and courage.

One of my primary objectives within this book is to bridge the gap between ancient prophecies and the complexities of our modern world. By drawing parallels between biblical foresight and present-day occurrences, you will gain insights into the unfolding events surrounding us. This connection illuminates the relevance and timeless wisdom of the Scriptures, empowering individuals to navigate the contemporary landscape with clarity and purpose.

In times of uncertainty, fear can grip our hearts, leaving us paralyzed and doubtful. *It's Midnight in America* serves as a guiding light, reminding us that hope can be found amidst the darkness. In these pages, you will discover that understanding prophecy can dissolve fear and instill hope, leading to a renewed sense of purpose and optimism.

Faith is an anchor that steadies us in the face of life's storms. This book serves as a catalyst for developing unshakable faith, grounded in the promises and truths of the Bible. By exploring biblical prophecy, you will gain a deeper understanding of God and strengthen your faith to withstand any trial—even at midnight.

Part I: A Look Back

THIS BOOK IS divided into four parts to provide some clear perspective on end-times events. First we'll take a look backward to get some retrospective context. Then in part II we'll look ahead to see what Scripture tells us we can expect to occur. Part III will challenge us to consider how we're living in between the certainties of the past and our expectations for the future. How are we doing as individuals and as a nation? Are we learning from the lessons of the past and watching for what's to come? Part IV will then address readiness. Since we know to a large extent what to expect, how do we prepare for it? We'll look at elements of a confident mindset that believers should develop in this midnight hour!

Specifically, in part I we'll start by looking back just a few years to consider how recent events may be more significant than many people realize. Then we'll go further back into our nation's history to acknowledge the respect and reverence shown by our Founding Fathers for faith and the Scripture as they created and organized a brand-new nation. Finally, we'll go back into ancient history as we follow the minute hand of the prophetic clock.

Various historical figures, including Winston Churchill and philosopher George Santayana, are quoted as saying, "Those that fail to learn from history are doomed to repeat it" (or some variation). We never want to forget that America has a blessed and impressive past. That's where we want to start.

Chapter 1

This Is a Dress Rehearsal

THE WORLD WITNESSED a momentous event in 2020 in the form of a global pandemic as governments around the world enacted strict measures to control the spread of COVID-19. Here in America, citizens found themselves grappling with the delicate balance between personal liberty and public safety. California was the first state to declare a statewide shelter-in-place order, yet as time passed doubts emerged regarding the government's handling of the crisis. Questions arose about the intentions behind such unprecedented restrictions. Was it wise for people to voluntarily give up their rights and freedoms? Whispers of possible manipulation began to circulate.

At Influence Church in Anaheim, California, we faced a pivotal decision when confronted with the prospect of closing our church and offices during the pandemic. We recognized that such measures were not in the best interests of our congregation and seemed to contradict our First Amendment rights under the US Constitution. Nevertheless, like many others, we attempted to comply with the newly imposed reality during those initial weeks, believing the government would act in our best interest and provide accurate information to protect us.

As time went on, our initial trust in the government's handling of the pandemic wavered. The daily barrage of reports predicting catastrophic death tolls from this relentless virus, along with the repeated mantra to "trust the science," left us uneasy. We felt an underlying suspicion that this phrase might be concealing something, raising concerns about potential manipulation and propaganda.

In reflecting on our growing doubts, the words of George Orwell, author of the iconic novel *1984*, came to mind. He aptly wrote, "We know that no one ever seizes power with the intention of relinquishing it."[1] This insightful observation made us question whether the government's actions were solely to protect the well-being of its citizens or if there were other motives at play.

Additionally, the wisdom of Martin Luther King Jr. resonated with us. He reminded us of the crucial role the church must play as the conscience of the state, serving as a guide and critic to uphold moral and spiritual values. However, it seemed that some churches were losing their prophetic zeal and becoming more like irrelevant social clubs, devoid of moral or spiritual authority. The challenging times demanded that churches stand firm in their convictions, operating in faith and refusing to be swayed by external pressures.

During that time, I came across a fascinating paper written in 1957 by social scientist Albert D. Biderman that detailed the eight steps of brainwashing utilized by Chinese and Korean interrogators to extract false confessions from US Air Force prisoners of war. Their tactics were designed to manipulate individuals' minds and emotions, ultimately rendering them psychological and physical captives.

Over time these eight steps were codified into a tool known as Biderman's Chart of Coercion,[2] serving to illustrate and explain the methods of stress manipulation employed. As I delved into the study of brainwashing techniques, it dawned on me that they bore a striking resemblance to the very strategy being employed on a global scale during the COVID-19 pandemic.

Below is a summary of Biderman's Chart of Coercion, and you can decide for yourself if it rings a familiar bell. I have included comments beneath each step to illustrate its application.

1. *Isolation*: Isolated individuals are deprived of any social support (lockdowns imposed during March 2020).

2. *Controlling Perception*: The narrative of a current problem is meticulously controlled to eliminate any information that contradicts the desired message. ("Wear two masks to minimize spread of contagion.")

3. *Humiliation*: This form of punishment heightens feelings of incompetence (shaming of nonconformists).

4. *Exhaustion*: Both physical and mental exhaustion are employed to quell resistance. ("A second wave is coming.")

5. *Threats*: Anxiety and despair are created through intimidation (fines, blocking on social media, and other penalties for not complying).

6. *Granting Occasional Indulgences*: Random rewards are given as a positive motivation for conforming to the demands of those in power. ("If you comply, you will be rewarded.")

7. *Power*: Position is imposed over individuals to convince them that resistance is futile. ("Follow the science.")

8. *Enforcing Trivial Demands*: The imposition of trivial and contradictory demands reinforces the control of those in authority (mask requirements and restaurant restrictions).

These steps from Biderman's Chart of Coercion reveal a chilling similarity to the methods employed during the pandemic, which should give us pause. They highlight a systematic approach to manipulate the population and erode personal freedoms under the guise of public health and safety. It is crucial to remain vigilant and uphold the principles that form the foundation of our society. Only by doing so can we ensure that our rights and freedoms are protected and our collective well-being is preserved.

BELIEVING VS. CONFORMING

It is essential to evaluate the actions of those in power, discerning whether they align with principles of transparency, accountability, and respect for individual liberties. In doing so, we can strive to safeguard our freedom and resist undue coercion. During the pandemic, everyone seemed to be debating where to draw the line between the need to minimize risk and the right to personal freedom.

One example was a thought-provoking exchange that unfolded during an interview of Governor Phil Murphy by Tucker Carlson. The New Jersey governor was defending his recent shutdowns of state parks and ban on large gatherings, including religious services. He emphasized reliance on data and science and had urged people to maintain physical distance. After Carlson cited an incident where fifteen congregants had been charged for assembling at a synagogue, he asked Murphy the crucial question "By what authority did you nullify the Bill of Rights?" Governor Murphy's accompanying statement was disconcerting: "That's above my pay grade, Tucker, so I wasn't thinking of the Bill of Rights when we did this." Carlson, undeterred, pressed further, questioning the governor's authority to order measures that seemingly contradicted constitutional rights.[3]

Simultaneously, across America the response from many churches was disheartening. They seemingly made science their guiding principle, with Dr. Fauci becoming their revered prophet. Church after church appeared to surrender to the prevailing narrative, adopting a passive stance. This passivity begged the question: Where was the power of Daniel, who bravely confronted King Darius' lions rather than abandon his regular practice of faith? Where was the unwavering faith of Shadrach, Meshach, and Abednego, who fearlessly faced Nebuchadnezzar's fury and the fiery furnace when they wouldn't bow to his statue?[4]

In their willingness to comply with government mandates, some churches seemed to forget the principles enshrined in the First Amendment. By allowing Caesar to reign over matters that should be within the domain of individual liberties, they inadvertently played into the hands of the government's increasing control. This paralleled the actions of the German church during Adolf Hitler's rise to power, which chose to align itself with the government rather than uphold its moral and spiritual authority.

History reminds us that when the church surrenders its core principles and authority, it risks becoming a passive instrument of control, perpetuating the very actions it should be opposing. Such historical events serve as a sobering reminder of the responsibility of religious institutions to remain vigilant in protecting fundamental freedoms and standing firm in their faith.

In January 2021 I was asked to do an interview with the *Epoch Times*, owing to our decision to open our church despite government mandates during the pandemic. During the pre-interview, I was asked about my experience in communist countries. I recounted an impactful event from 1990 when my wife and I went to Romania. Despite the fall of the Berlin Wall in 1989 and the subsequent execution of dictator Nicolae Ceausescu on Christmas Day the same year, the Romanian government remained under a veil of oppression, curbing the advancement of Christianity. We determined to smuggle Bibles into the country. We had carefully removed the lining of our suitcases, discreetly concealed as many New Testaments as we could, and glued the lining back into place. Though we were amateurs in the world of smuggling, we believed our determination to share the Word of God outweighed the risks.

At the airport, a moment of tension arose when the attendant checking our luggage questioned us about any forbidden items, specifically mentioning Bibles. Uncertain of how to respond truthfully without jeopardizing our mission, we hesitated. In a fortuitous twist, a supervisor intervened, seemingly prepared to expose our actions. However, to our astonishment, he revealed himself as a fellow Christian and asked, "There are Bibles in your luggage, aren't there?" Without hesitation, I confirmed his suspicion, to which he responded, "I'm going to approve your luggage all the way to Belgrade, Yugoslavia." This unexpected encounter was a testament to the power of divine intervention and the ways in which faith can bridge unexpected connections.

I also described another life-changing experience while doing crusades in El Salvador amid the backdrop of the civil war between the government and the communist FMLN party. During that tumultuous period, I witnessed scenes of revolt, tear gassing, and people being threatened and shot. Yet, amidst the chaos, I also saw the profound power of God in bringing salvation to thousands of individuals who were hungry for the gospel message. It was an undeniable affirmation of the strength of faith, even in the darkest of times.

During the interview, one question stood out: "Do you see any similarities between the church in China and the USA?" I felt an undeniable guidance from the Holy Spirit as I confidently replied, "Yes, China has a state church and an underground church. In America, we now have the *conforming* church and the *believing* church." This observation drew a parallel between the challenges faced by religious institutions in both countries where some choose to conform to prevailing norms while others, like us, uphold their convictions and principles.

Reflecting on my experiences and the subsequent interview, I realized the profound impact of standing firm in one's faith, especially in the face of adversity. It was a reminder that the power of God transcends borders and that faith remains a source of unwavering strength in turbulent times. As we navigate through ever-changing circumstances, I am resolved to uphold the values of the believing church and continue striving to inspire hope, compassion, and a steadfast commitment to our faith.

RUN WITH THE HORSES

Seeing how many pastors in California chose to comply with government mandates and close their church doors was disheartening. Simultaneously, they criticized those who decided to remain open, labeling them as potential "super-spreaders" who neglected their neighbors' well-being. Based on my observation, out of the more than thirty thousand churches in California, fewer than 10 percent chose to open their doors during the lockdown.

A few churches were quick to abandon public gatherings altogether in pursuit of a different model for church that didn't include group singing, worship, or interpersonal fellowship. Others sought a middle-ground solution. One near us created large outdoor circles for their services. Attendees were required to remain within their designated circles and not engage in "fellowship" with others outside their circle. They even went to the extent of setting up COVID vaccine stations on the church premises and mandated masks for all.

Influence Church was in the minority. We determined to stand strong in our decision to remain open. As a result, our church faced adversity and was even labeled "Influenza" Church by a neighboring megachurch that had chosen to close. We faced harassment and were reported to OSHA (the Occupational Safety and Health Administration) for allegedly violating requirements. Nevertheless, we stood firm, witnessing the emergence of a new caliber of Christian—battle-hardened and prepared to face the trials of persecution. I could sense in my spirit that this was merely a dress rehearsal for what the church will face in the last days.

As coming trials loom on the horizon, it is likely that many churches will falter. Only the believing church, deeply rooted in faith, will be able to stand firm. The conforming churches, reminiscent of the Lutheran Church's stance under the Nazi regime, are likely to falter and fold.

It's disheartening to see that some conforming church pastors have chosen to ignore their failure to take a stand when it was most needed. Instead, they continue with business as usual, justifying their lack of courage under the guise of protecting their congregation. However, the people have not forgotten those choices and the consequences they may bear. The COVID pandemic appears to be just the beginning of what may befall our planet. We will see in later chapters how sinister and powerful individuals scheme to use any opportunity to strip away personal freedoms and wealth and gain more control over every aspect of our lives. How we respond will define the course of our future.

In conclusion, the words of Jeremiah the prophet echo across time, posing a poignant question that remains relevant today: "If you have run with the footmen, and they have wearied you, then how can you contend with horses?" (Jer. 12:5). This thought, resonating through the ages, urges us to reflect on our ability to withstand greater challenges in the face of adversity.

Geoffrey Chaucer's words from the *Canterbury Tales* further illuminate this sentiment, warning us about the consequences of neglecting our responsibilities: "If the gold rusts, what will become of the iron, and if the priests fail, what will happen to the people?" The parallels between these historical reflections and our current circumstances serve as cautionary reminders of the impact of our choices and actions.

Congregants look to their leaders for guidance and inspiration, especially during times of uncertainty and crisis. Unfortunately, many conforming church pastors have chosen to overlook their failure to stand strong when it was most needed. Instead of rising to the occasion and protecting their congregations, they have opted for business as usual. They may have short memories, but the people don't. The choices made by pastors reverberate throughout their communities and shape the moral fabric of society.

As we move forward, it is essential to remain vigilant, informed, and grounded in our values. We must recognize the schemes of those who seek to manipulate and control us while also acknowledging the potential for good in the world. Evil will always be present, but how much more so the resilience and strength available through the power of God. Faith, hope, and love can overcome even the darkest of times.

In the upcoming chapters, we will delve into the enemy's master plan, deciphering its intricacies and unveiling its potential impact on our lives. Equipped with knowledge and discernment, we can stand firm against the encroaching darkness and protect what is most precious—our faith, our freedoms, and our future.

It is imperative to remember the lessons of history, drawing strength from the faith of those who faced tribulations before us. We find inspiration in the courage and determination of Daniel, Shadrach, Meshach, Abednego, and other heroes of the past. By upholding the principles of truth, justice, and compassion, we can emerge as a powerful force against tyranny and oppression.

The journey ahead may be challenging, but united in our pursuit of freedom and justice, we can overcome any obstacle. Let us remain steadfast in our faith, true to our beliefs, and strong in our resolve to protect what is sacred and dear to us. Together we can break free from the snares of the devil's plan and forge a path toward a brighter and more promising future. May our journey through the darkest of times be guided by the light of truth, leading us toward a world where freedom, equality, and love prevail. And in this pursuit, let us never forget that we are not alone. The spirit of goodness and righteousness resides within each one of us. Let it be the beacon that guides us through the storm, illuminating our way toward a better tomorrow.

Chapter 2

An Appeal to Heaven

AN ARTICLE IN a psychology magazine had an intriguing opening. The authors asked, "Whether it's moving house, planning a wedding, or putting together a killer pitch to land a major client, how many times have you found yourself faced with a task that seems so overwhelming that your brain freezes in blind panic?...If Insta, TikTok and Netflix don't cut it, what *should* you do when you're faced with a task of seemingly impossible magnitude? The answer is, turn to GOD!"

Surprised? When was the last time you heard of a psychological organization offering spiritual advice for a problem of disorientation and stress? Well, before you become too impressed, keep reading. After describing some of their own personal achievements, the authors explained: "The success of the venture depended in no small part on our strict adherence to an omnipotent code of psychological conduct that we call the 'GOD Principle'. 'GOD' stands for guts, organisation, and determination, and with GOD on your side, we believe you can achieve pretty much anything you set your mind to in life, no matter how big or small it might be."[1]

Set aside for the moment any concern you might have that

this wordplay may be taking the Lord's name in vain. Instead, let's take a closer look at what the authors have done. They have admitted publicly to the strategy that so many others follow much more subtly, perhaps even imperceptibly. They have replaced the readily available wisdom and power of the almighty God with a strategy of purely human effort. Undoubtedly, their advice will be quite effective much of the time. After all, a combination of guts, organization, and determination is the basic game plan of every coach of every sport.

Yet when more is at stake than merely persevering through a physical test of strength, or planning a wedding, or selling a concept to a client, sometimes no amount of human effort is sufficient. Sometimes the solution is to stop believing that we can muster enough willpower to do everything on our own, quit fighting a losing battle, and humbly ask God to do what only He can do for us. Let's look at several examples of individuals who had more than their fair share of guts, organization, and determination yet knew when it was time to look to a higher power for solutions beyond their own capabilities. We'll start with a few historic examples.

PATRICK HENRY

In the tumultuous year of 1775, the American colonies found themselves on the precipice of an unprecedented struggle for freedom and self-determination. It was in this pivotal moment that Patrick Henry, a fiery orator and one of the Founding Fathers of the United States, delivered his famous "Give me liberty or give me death" speech in Richmond, Virginia. But prior to that often-quoted closing statement, he declared with impassioned fervor, "An appeal to arms and to the God of hosts is all that is left us!...We shall not fight our battles alone. There is a just God who presides over the destinies of nations...."[2] These words, etched into the annals of history, resonate with timeless wisdom and courage.

The American colonists, driven by a burning desire for liberty and self-governance, had exhausted every diplomatic avenue. The oppressive measures imposed by the British Crown had pushed them to a breaking point, leaving them with a stark choice: submission or resistance. At its core, Henry's declaration was a call to arms, a rallying cry for a people who had endured oppression and injustice, and who had come to a crossroads where peaceful reconciliation seemed increasingly elusive. In invoking "the God of hosts," Patrick Henry was drawing upon a deep well of religious conviction that permeated the hearts and minds of many colonists.

The American Revolution was not merely a political struggle; it was seen by many as a divine mission. Henry believed their cause was just, and that the Almighty, as the ultimate arbiter of justice, would stand with those who sought freedom from tyranny.

Henry's words were a powerful reminder that the colonists were not alone in their struggle. They believed in the providence of a higher power, a God who watched over the affairs of nations. This faith imbued them with the strength to confront the daunting challenges that lay ahead. It gave them the resolve to face a formidable adversary, the British Empire, with its vast resources and military might.

Moreover, Henry's assertion that "we shall not fight our battles alone" was a testament to the unity and collective spirit of the American people. They were not disparate colonies but a burgeoning nation, bound together by a shared vision of independence. In their collective efforts, they found strength and determination that transcended individual limitations.

The phrase "the God of hosts" hearkens to a biblical tradition where God is depicted as a divine warrior leading the righteous to victory. The original word for the *hosts* of heaven invokes an image of a heavenly *army*. This imagery resonated deeply with the colonists, who saw themselves as fighting for a just and righteous cause. It bolstered their morale and instilled in them a sense of divine purpose.

Patrick Henry's words continue to echo through the corridors of American history, reminding us of the profound faith and resolve that fueled the American Revolution. They serve as a testament to the power of faith, unity, and belief in a just cause. Henry's call to arms encapsulates the spirit of a young nation determined to chart its own destiny, even in the face of overwhelming odds.

Henry's proclamation was not just a call to war; it was a plea to uphold the principles of liberty and justice, even when the path forward was uncertain. It was a reminder that, in times of great challenge, faith in a just God and the collective strength of a united people can illuminate the darkest of days and pave the way to a brighter future. Patrick Henry's words remain an ongoing testament to the enduring power of hope, faith, and the indomitable human spirit.

JOHN LOCKE

Patrick Henry may have drawn from the work of John Locke, a prominent philosopher of the Enlightenment era. Locke's writings from the 1690s articulated a profound perspective on the relationship between the rights of the people, justice, and the ultimate authority of God. Locke's words encapsulate a fundamental principle of natural rights philosophy and resonate with the inherent dignity and agency of individuals.

In Locke's view, when people are systematically deprived of their rights and lack any recourse or appeal on earth, they possess the liberty to "appeal to Heaven."[3] This concept of appealing to a higher authority underscores a belief in the universality of human rights that transcends any earthly jurisdiction. It implies that when individuals are subjected to oppression or injustice without the means to seek redress within their society, they can turn to a higher moral authority for vindication.

Locke's assertion that there may be situations where "there lies no appeal on Earth"[4] further emphasizes the gravity of the circumstances under which individuals may invoke divine intervention. When human institutions and systems fail to protect the rights and liberties of the people, they are left with no other recourse than to place their trust in a higher power.

The core of Locke's argument lies in the assertion that "where there is no [justice] on Earth, to decide controversies amongst men, God in Heaven is Judge."[5] This declaration aligns with the belief that ultimate justice resides in a higher moral order, beyond the limitations of human judgment and institutions. It underscores the idea that when earthly systems fail to uphold justice and protect the rights of individuals, there remains a higher standard of justice by which actions can be measured.

Locke concludes by suggesting that in such circumstances, individuals should "appeal to the Supreme Judge." This symbolizes an act of moral conviction and a plea for divine intervention to rectify injustices. It reflects the human spirit's capacity to seek justice, even when faced with seemingly insurmountable challenges and obstacles.[6]

DANIEL WEBSTER

Daniel Webster, a renowned American statesman and orator of the nineteenth century, was deemed one of the five greatest senators in US history (called the "Famous Five") by a resolution of the Senate.[7] Many of his speeches called his listeners to a greater respect for God and country. Here are a few examples:

God grants liberty only to those who love it, and are always ready to guard and defend it.[8]

By the blessing of God, may [our] country itself become a vast and splendid monument, not of oppression and terror, but of wisdom, of peace, and of liberty, upon which the world may gaze with admiration forever!"[9]

The Constitution has enemies, secret and professed.... They have hot heads and cold hearts. They are rash, reckless, and fierce for change, and with no affection for the existing institutions of their country. Other enemies there are, more cool, and with more calculation. These have a deeper and more fixed and dangerous purpose....There are those in the country, who profess, in their own words, even to hate the Constitution.[10]

Webster's words serve as a solemn reminder of the responsibilities that come with the precious gift of liberty and the duty to preserve the legacy handed down to us by our forebears. In contemplating these words, we must ask ourselves whether the spirit of liberty still courses through our veins, as it did for our revolutionary forefathers. Have we, the inheritors of their hard-fought freedoms, remained vigilant and committed to safeguarding the principles upon which our nation was founded? The world indeed would cry "Shame on you!" if we were to prove unworthy of our lineage. The sacrifices made by the men who fought and died for liberty, and the legacy of freedom they secured for us through the Constitution, stand as a testament to their dedication to the cause of liberty.

Yet, as Webster noted, there are forces both secret and professed that harbor ill intentions toward our Constitution. These adversaries of our foundational document may be driven by a reckless desire for change, and they may lack the reverence and affection for the institutions that have upheld our nation's values for over two centuries. Some even openly express their hatred for the Constitution. In the face of such challenges, Webster implores us to rally and unite as defenders of the Constitution. He calls upon us to stand firm and resolute, akin to a band of brothers, with an unwavering commitment to preserve this precious inheritance from our ancestors.

Preserving the Constitution is not a passive endeavor; it requires dedication and vigilance. In an ever-changing world, the enemies of the Constitution may advocate for radical and hasty alterations. They may seek to undermine the very foundations that have allowed our nation to thrive. However, as guardians of the Constitution, we must remain steadfast in our resolve to protect the liberties it guarantees.

Webster emphasizes the importance of setting aside our differences when defending the Constitution. Regardless of our individual beliefs or political affiliations, the preservation of our foundational document must be our common cause. It is the duty of every citizen, irrespective of their background or ideology, to ensure that the Constitution endures for future generations.

In an era marked by division and polarization, the imperative to unite in defense of our Constitution becomes even more critical. We must transcend partisan divides and prioritize the greater good of our nation. The Constitution is not a mere legal document; it represents the aspirations of a people who sought to create a just and free society. It embodies the dreams and sacrifices of those who came before us.

As we reflect on Daniel Webster's words, we are reminded that the struggle to preserve liberty is ongoing. The enemies of the Constitution may change over time, but the duty to defend it remains constant. It is a duty that we owe to our forefathers, to ourselves, and to future generations.

The Prophet Isaiah

When we appeal to heaven, seeking God's help for a particularly trying circumstance or desperate need, God often responds by appealing to us. He may suggest specific actions we can take to address the issue that concerns us, because it probably concerns others as well.

In Isaiah 58, God's people have appealed to Him because He hasn't responded to their efforts to impress Him with their spiritual devotion. God saw through their token attempts at fasting and trying to appear humble. Their fasting wasn't taking them closer to God; it was only making them hangry and causing them to take out their discomfort on one another. God appealed to them to stop their malicious criticism of one another and start sharing their food with the hungry and providing for the poor. If they did so, God made several promises of what they could expect from Him. Several are listed in Isaiah 58:12:

> Those from among you shall build the old waste places; you shall raise up the foundations of many generations; and you shall be called the Repairer of the Breach, the Restorer of Streets to Dwell In.

This verse carries profound wisdom that transcends time and speaks directly to our sense of purpose and destiny. Isaiah paints a vivid picture of the potential within each of us. He speaks to the idea that we have a divine calling and responsibility, and he conveys God's powerful message about our role in shaping the world around us and leaving a lasting legacy for future generations. Let's look more closely at these promises and challenges.

- "Those from among you shall build the old waste places."

This statement signifies a call to action. It encourages us to look at the neglected, forgotten, or deteriorated aspects of our world and take steps to rebuild and restore them. In practical terms, it may refer to revitalizing decaying communities, preserving cultural heritage, or even mending broken relationships or healing a nation torn apart by sin and confusion.

- "You shall raise up the foundations of many generations."

  This line speaks to the enduring impact of our actions. By addressing the foundational issues and challenges of our time, we have the opportunity to create a legacy that will benefit not only our generation but also others yet to come. It emphasizes the importance of forward thinking and long-term planning in our endeavors.

- "And you shall be called the Repairer of the Breach, the Restorer of Streets to Dwell In."

  Here Isaiah assigns titles to those who embrace this divine calling. "Repairer of the Breach" suggests that we have the power to mend divisions, bridge gaps, and heal wounds in society. It underscores our capacity to promote unity and harmony. "Restorer of Streets to Dwell In" evokes the image of creating safe and welcoming communities where people can live, work, and thrive. It reminds us of the role we can play in making the world a better place for all.

Isaiah 58:12 challenges us to consider our purpose and impact on the world around us. It calls us to action, urging us to take responsibility for the well-being of our communities and the legacy we leave behind. Whether through acts of kindness, environmental stewardship, or efforts to promote social justice, this verse encourages us to become active participants in the betterment of our world.

Our destiny, as illuminated by this verse, is not passive but active. It is about intentionally engaging with the world's challenges and working toward solutions. It's about recognizing that we have the power to make a positive difference in our communities and beyond. It emphasizes the importance of leaving behind a world that future generations can be proud of—a legacy of healing, restoration, and unity.

As we look back across history, we find numerous examples of men and women who, under very strenuous circumstances, faced their trying times with great courage, tenacity, and perseverance. More importantly, they knew the importance of appealing to God to achieve personal victory they never could have accomplished on their own. More recently, however, it seems that such people are becoming harder to find. So let's now look at a few contemporary people with suggestions for how to maintain ultimate trust in God as a priority.

A SPIRITUAL BATTLE, HERE AND NOW

Richard Booker is a Christian minister who founded a ministry to help Christians better understand the Hebraic culture and background of the Bible, and to promote better understanding between Christians and Jews. He is also a writer who has concentrated much of his attention on the Book of Revelation and the end times. Booker connects the seen with the unseen as he reminds us, "We cannot see this mystery of God and this great end-time spiritual battle taking place with our physical eyes. It is all happening in the heaven or spiritual realm."[11]

We must have spiritual eyes to have an awareness of what's taking place "behind the scenes" of what we witness through our physical eyes and ears. Yet we get a good indication by seeing the impact of the spiritual struggle as it affects the earth. What is happening in the spiritual realm is manifested physically, and we'll see it if we're paying attention.

Booker beckons us to peer beyond the veil of our physical world and delve into the unseen realm of spiritual warfare. He challenges us to develop spiritual discernment, for the battles that unfold are not visible to our physical eyes but are instead waged in the spiritual domain. Booker's words invite us to contemplate the profound interplay between the spiritual and physical dimensions and how the spiritual realm shapes the course of human history.

In the realm of spirituality, the concept of an end-time spiritual battle holds deep significance. It alerts us to a coming cosmic struggle of immense proportions, a spiritual clash between forces of light and darkness. To comprehend this spiritual battle, one must possess spiritual eyes that can perceive the unseen world. This is biblical language signifying the need for heightened spiritual awareness and insight. It suggests that our understanding of reality must transcend the material and tangible, reaching into the depths of the spiritual.

Booker's assertion that we can gauge the unfolding spiritual battle by observing its impact on the physical world underscores the interconnectedness of these two realms. In essence, he proposes that the spiritual realm, though invisible, manifests itself tangibly in our lives and the world around us.

Consider, for instance, the societal unrest, moral decay, and conflicts that plague our world. From Booker's perspective, these manifestations are not solely the result of political, economic, or social factors; they are also reflections of the spiritual battle occurring behind the scenes. In times of conflict, turmoil, and moral ambiguity, we witness the outward manifestations of deeper spiritual struggles.

The apostle Paul confirms this: "For we do not wrestle against flesh and blood, but against principalities, against powers, against the rulers of the darkness of this age, against spiritual hosts of wickedness in the heavenly places" (Eph. 6:12). This biblical passage underscores the notion that human conflicts are not purely of this world but are influenced by spiritual forces.

Understanding the spiritual battle as an end-time phenomenon adds an eschatological dimension to Booker's statement. It suggests that this ongoing spiritual conflict will intensify and culminate in a final confrontation between good and evil, light and darkness, truth and deception.

Booker's words also serve as a call to action. If we accept the existence of this end-time spiritual battle, it compels us to be vigilant and proactive in our spiritual lives. It encourages us to seek spiritual wisdom, practice discernment, and engage in prayer and meditation to gain a deeper understanding of the spiritual forces at play.

Moreover, recognizing the spiritual battle's impact on the physical world challenges us to be agents of positive change. We become participants in the ongoing struggle by promoting justice, compassion, and righteousness in our communities. Instead of resigning to a passive role, we are inspired to actively contribute to the betterment of our world, aligning our actions with the forces of light and goodness.

THE POWER OF THE CROSS OF CALVARY

Paul Billheimer was a longtime radio pastor and teacher who appears to agree with Booker. In his book *Destined for the Throne*, Billheimer writes that we are confronted with the idea that the church of the living God stands as the sole force opposing the potential reign of darkness and chaos in human affairs orchestrated by Satan:

> The only force in the world that is contesting Satan's total rule in human affairs is the Church of the living God. If Satan were unopposed, if he were under no restraint because of the Spirit-inspired prayers and holy lives of God's people, "the pillared firmament itself were rottenness and earth's base built on stubble." If there were nothing to hinder him, Satan would make a hell out of this world here and now. The only saving and healing virtue in the howling deserts of human life flows from the cross of Calvary. The only pure unselfishness in the world issues from the fountain filled with blood. If it were not for the totally selfless love displayed on the bloody cross, total selfishness would reign supreme. And total selfishness means total hostility. Total hostility means total anarchy—*and that means hell.*[12]

Billheimer's assertion is that without the presence of the church and its commitment to upholding the teachings of Christ, the world would be much more susceptible to the malevolent influence of Satan. In this view, the church serves as a beacon of light and hope in a world that would otherwise descend into moral and spiritual decay. This perspective delves into the realm of spiritual warfare, highlighting the pivotal role that faith and the redemptive power of the cross play in the ongoing battle between good and evil.

The notion that Satan would turn the world into a living hell underscores the magnitude of the spiritual battle unfolding. It suggests that the forces of evil are ceaselessly working to corrupt humanity and undermine the values of compassion, love, and righteousness. In this context, the church's mission becomes clear: to combat the darkness with the radiant message of salvation and redemption.

The reference to "the cross of Calvary" is central to Billheimer's message. It symbolizes the ultimate sacrifice made by Jesus Christ for the salvation of humanity. The cross is not only a symbol of suffering but also a powerful emblem of hope, forgiveness, and divine love. It represents how individuals can find redemption, forgiveness of sins, and eternal life.

Billheimer's words inspire reflection on the role of faith and spirituality in navigating the complexities of human existence. They remind us of the enduring battle between good and evil that transcends the physical world and extends into the spiritual realm. In this context, the church is seen as a force for good, standing as a bulwark against the destructive influence of darkness.

Ultimately, Paul Billheimer's statement calls upon believers to recognize the significance of their faith and the responsibility it carries. It underscores the idea that the teachings of Christ and the redemptive power of the cross provide a path toward salvation, healing, and the restoration of human souls. In a world where moral and spiritual challenges abound, the church remains a shining light in the struggle against the forces that seek to undermine the well-being of humanity.

THE COMPANY YOU KEEP

Andy Andrews, a popular speaker and best-selling author, offers sage advice through his characters and storytelling. One observation he makes is to "Guard your associations carefully....Anytime you tolerate mediocrity in your choice of companions, you become more comfortable with mediocrity in your own life."[13] Andrews' insight speaks volumes about the profound impact our relationships and associations can have on our personal growth, aspirations, and overall quality of life. This powerful message underscores the importance of surrounding ourselves with people who inspire us, challenge us, and elevate us to become our best selves.

In a world filled with diverse personalities and influences, other people play a pivotal role in shaping our character and determining the trajectory of our lives. Our associations encompass not only our friendships but also our mentors, colleagues, and acquaintances. Each connection we forge contributes to the tapestry of our experiences and ultimately influences the person we become.

At its core, Andrews' advice urges us to be discerning in our choice of companions. It encourages us to seek out individuals who exemplify excellence, ambition, and integrity. When we surround ourselves with people who set high standards for themselves, we are more likely to adopt those same standards in our own lives. Conversely, tolerating mediocrity in our associations can inadvertently lower our own expectations and aspirations.

Consider the principle of "the company you keep." When we spend time with people who excel in their chosen fields, whether it be in academics, sports, art, or business, we witness the dedication, discipline, and hard work required to achieve greatness. Such exposure can serve as a powerful motivator, inspiring us to pursue our own goals with greater zeal and determination. Conversely, if we surround ourselves with those who settle for mediocrity, we may find ourselves growing complacent and comfortable, with less-than-stellar performance. It's not that we consciously choose to lower our standards; rather, it's a gradual process that occurs subconsciously as we assimilate the attitudes and values of those around us.

This phenomenon extends beyond our professional and academic lives. It influences our personal development, emotional well-being, and even our moral compass. The friends we confide in, the mentors we seek guidance from, and the role models we admire all contribute to our sense of self and the choices we make. Moreover, the impact of our associations extends to our ability to overcome challenges and face adversity. When we surround ourselves with individuals who exhibit courage, resilience, and a can-do attitude, we are more likely to adopt those qualities ourselves. And their support and belief in our capabilities can bolster our confidence in times of uncertainty.

On the other hand, if we find ourselves in the company of those who succumb to fear, doubt, or defeatism, we may struggle to summon the strength to confront life's obstacles. Our associations can either fortify our resolve or weaken our spirit, depending on the prevailing attitudes and mindsets of those we choose to align ourselves with.

Andrews' message also applies to the ability to quiet our fears and stand with courage. The individuals we surround ourselves with can either fuel our fears or embolden our bravery. A supportive and encouraging network of friends, mentors, and allies can provide us with the confidence and resilience needed to confront our fears and pursue our aspirations.

Quieting our fears and standing with courage is seldom a solitary endeavor. It is a collective effort that thrives in the presence of positive influences and unwavering support. When we choose our companions wisely, we create a network of allies who can bolster our courage, offer guidance, and serve as a source of inspiration when the path ahead seems daunting.

Quietly silencing our fears doesn't imply suppressing or

denying them. Instead, it requires acknowledging our fears, understanding their origins, and confronting them with resilience and determination. It demands that we stand tall in the face of adversity, resolute in our commitment to pursue our dreams and aspirations.

Courage, often described as the ability to act in the face of fear, is a quality that can be cultivated and nurtured. When we embrace courage, we become agents of change in our own lives. We discover the strength to step out of our comfort zones, take risks, and confront challenges head-on.

NEW FEARS

We face new challenges that previous generations did not. Joy Pullmann, author and executive editor of *The Federalist*, raises critical concerns about the potential emergence of a nongovernmental social credit system in formerly free nations like the United States. This system, she argues, bears resemblance to the one employed by Communist China, where individuals are economically and socially penalized for "wrongthink" (holding views contrary to those endorsed by the government). Pullman suggests that global oligarchs are collaborating with China to export this system of social control to free societies. She says:

> The social credit system in China basically applies economic pressure to coerce people into behaving the way that the totalitarian government wants them to....If you have a low credit score in China, you can't bank, you can't travel, your kids can't go to a good school. All sorts of things that this crazy cancel-culture, and mobs on the left are already pressuring here in the United States....We have been internally seeing censorship applied to our platform at *The Federalist*.[14]

The notion of a social credit system is indeed alarming, as it implies a level of surveillance and control over individual beliefs and behaviors that infringes upon the principles of liberty and autonomy cherished in democratic nations. The comparison to China's system is particularly concerning, given its well-documented violations of human rights and suppression of dissenting voices. (We'll see more about this in chapter 4.)

Pullmann's concern is further illustrated by the remarks attributed to PBS attorney Michael Beller, who allegedly spoke about targeting Republican voters and threatening to separate their children and place them in reeducation camps.[15] While PBS disavowed Beller's statements and emphasized that he did not represent the organization's values, his comments raise questions about the potential consequences of extreme political polarization and the erosion of civil discourse.

However, it is essential to approach such claims with discernment and to seek verifiable information before drawing conclusions. In an era marked by the proliferation of misinformation and the politicization of news, critical thinking and responsible journalism are more crucial than ever. While the concerns raised by Pullmann and others warrant attention and scrutiny, it is also essential to maintain a balanced perspective and avoid perpetuating unfounded conspiracy theories.

All of us undergo trying times and difficult circumstances, and they are likely to increase in our current culture of chaos fueled by greed, lust for power, and other self-centered motivations. Believers need to never forget that we have choices. When faced with some of these new fears—especially those you can't personally prevent or improve—you can rant, you can weep, you can protest, or you can pull the bedcovers up over your head. And then, when none of those options work, always remember that you can appeal to heaven. In fact, the sooner you learn to just skip those former options and go straight to the latter one, the sooner you will see that God can accomplish positive changes in your life (and maybe even in the world around you) that you could never change on your own.

I think Zechariah the prophet said it best: "'Not by might nor by power, but by My Spirit,' says the LORD of hosts" (Zech. 4:6). What more could we ask for?

Chapter 3

The Prophetic Clock

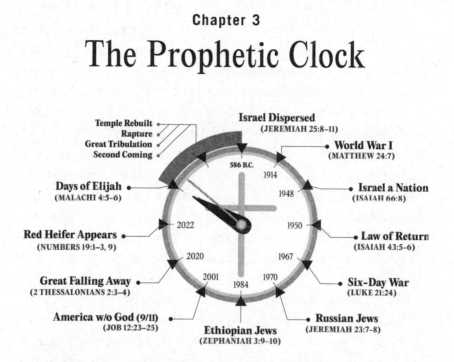

YOU'VE PROBABLY HEARD about the Doomsday Clock. It was created in 1947 as an indicator of how close our planet is getting to "midnight"—global catastrophe. At its origin, the Doomsday Clock was set to seven minutes before midnight. The greatest danger at that time came from nuclear weapons and the cold war between the United States and the Soviet Union. Indeed, by 1953, atomic scientists had advanced the minute hand to two minutes before midnight. In its seventy-six years of existence, the clock has only been reset twenty-five times. The most optimistic of those changes was 1991 when it was set back to seventeen minutes before midnight. But with recent unsettling world events and climate issues, the most recent change was in 2023 when the clock was set at ninety seconds before midnight—as close as it's ever been.[1]

In this chapter we want to look at a different timepiece: a *prophetic* clock. The prophetic clock marks prophecies of Jesus and several Old Testament prophets (some fulfilled and others yet to come) regarding the approach of God's plan for the end of the age. The idea of a prophetic clock is found in the teachings of Jesus in the Gospels. In Matthew 24, Mark 13, and Luke 21, Jesus describes various signs and events that will precede His second coming and the end of the age. These signs include wars, famines, earthquakes, persecution of believers, false prophets, and a great falling away from the faith. Ultimately, the concept of the prophetic clock should lead believers to a deeper sense of anticipation and preparedness for the return of Jesus Christ.

Jesus Himself encouraged His followers to watch for the signs that serve as markers for His coming (Matt. 24:42–44). The prophetic clock reminds us to look back and see that God's plan is unfolding according to His divine timetable and to look to the future as we live faithfully, prayerfully, and with an eternal perspective in the present age. Let's look now at some already fulfilled events on the prophetic clock.

ISRAEL DISPERSED (586 BC)

The prophecy:

> Therefore thus says the LORD of hosts: "Because you have not heard My words, behold, I will send and take all the families of the north," says the LORD, "and Nebuchadnezzar the king

of Babylon, My servant, and will bring them against this land, against its inhabitants, and against these nations all around, and will utterly destroy them, and make them an astonishment, a hissing, and perpetual desolations. Moreover I will take from them the voice of mirth and the voice of gladness, the voice of the bridegroom and the voice of the bride, the sound of the millstones and the light of the lamp. And this whole land shall be a desolation and an astonishment, and these nations shall serve the king of Babylon seventy years."

—JEREMIAH 25:8–11

The year 586 BC marked a critical juncture in Israel's history when the Babylonians conquered Jerusalem and destroyed the first temple. This event led to the exile of the Jewish people, known as the Babylonian captivity, or the Diaspora. The dispersion of Israel was a fulfillment of the prophetic warnings given by various prophets, including Jeremiah and Ezekiel.

For years Israel had failed to remain faithful to God, engaging in idolatry and social injustice. Because of their persistent disobedience, God allowed the Babylonians to invade and take control of their land. The destruction of the temple was a terrible blow to Israel's national and religious identity, forcing the Jewish people to endure a difficult period of exile and displacement.

The Babylonian captivity marked a turning point for Israel. It was a time of national introspection and soul-searching. During their time in exile, the Jewish people longed for their homeland and repented for their past sins. It was during this period that many foundations of Jewish identity, including the study of the Torah and the development of synagogues, were established. The exile also laid the groundwork for the eventual return to the land of Israel.

World War I (1914–1917)

The prophecy:

> For nation will rise against nation, and kingdom against kingdom.
>
> —Matthew 24:7

One of the most profound correlations made in modern history is between these prophetic words spoken by Jesus and the devastating events of World War I. The Great War, as it was known at the time, was truly unprecedented in its scale and devastation. Commencing in 1914, it was supposed to be the "war to end all wars." Yet what it showcased was humanity's ability to unleash destruction on an unimaginable scale. Major European powers, bound by a complex web of alliances and treaties, quickly became embroiled in a conflict that would span continents. This was not just a regional skirmish or a battle of empires; it was a global catastrophe where nations and kingdoms truly rose against each other.

When analyzing the context of Matthew 24:7, Jesus' words were in response to questions about the end times and the signs of His coming. His descriptions were of events so catastrophic they would herald the end of the age. In this light, the events of World War I can indeed be viewed as a precursor or warning sign of even more significant events yet to come. The scale of destruction, the uprooting of old-world orders, and the profound shifts in international dynamics all point to Jesus' prophecy.

Moreover, as nations tried to rebuild, the aftermath of World War I was marked by significant geopolitical, socioeconomic, and cultural changes. The Treaty of Versailles, which was meant to formalize peace and prevent future conflicts, ended up doing quite the opposite. The punitive measures against Germany, the carving out of new nations without regard to ethnic or religious affiliations, and the immense economic burdens placed on many countries only sowed the seeds for another global conflict just a couple of decades later.

In many ways, World War I shook the very foundations of human civilization. Empires that had lasted centuries collapsed. Monarchies were overthrown as new ideologies, from Communism to Fascism, began to take root. Technology too played a role, with advancements in warfare leading to more efficient ways to kill and destroy. Humanity was at a crossroads, with old systems failing and new ones yet to be tested.

The relationship between World War I and biblical prophecy underscores the enduring power of Scripture to illuminate, guide, and predict the future.

Israel's Rebirth as a Nation (May 14, 1948)

The prophecy:

> Who has heard such a thing? Who has seen such things? Shall the earth be made to give birth in one day? Or shall a nation be born at once? For as soon as Zion was in labor, she gave birth to her children.
>
> —Isaiah 66:8

After centuries of exile, persecution, and Israel's yearning for their homeland, the prophetic clock began to move toward the remarkable moment when they would be reborn as a nation. The Jewish people's yearning for their homeland had seen fruition with the start of the Zionist movement in the late nineteenth century. The dream of returning to Zion, their ancestral land, became a driving force for Jews worldwide. That momentous event occurred on May 14, 1948, when David Ben-Gurion, the head of the Jewish Agency, proclaimed the establishment of the State of Israel.

The United States played a pivotal role in recognizing Israel's sovereignty, and the United Nations' approval further legitimized its existence on the international stage. Within a twenty-four-hour span of being recognized as a nation, Israel had a declaration of independence and the acknowledgment of other countries, signifying the fulfillment of biblical prophecies that spoke of Israel's swift and sudden rebirth. A nation was born in a day.

THE LAW OF RETURN (JULY 5, 1950)

The prophecy:

> I will bring your descendants from the east, and gather you from the west; I will say to the north, "Give them up!" And to the south, "Do not keep them back!" Bring My sons from afar, and My daughters from the ends of the earth.
>
> —ISAIAH 43:5–6

The Law of Return was enacted by the Knesset (the Israeli parliament) on July 5, 1950, granting Jews around the world the right to immigrate to Israel and obtain citizenship. It played a crucial role in shaping the demographics of modern Israel as Jews came "from afar"—from all around the world—as a manifestation of divine providence and God's faithfulness to His covenant.

THE SIX-DAY WAR (JUNE 5–10, 1967)

The prophecy:

> And they will fall by the edge of the sword, and be led away captive into all nations. And Jerusalem will be trampled by Gentiles until the times of the Gentiles are fulfilled.
>
> —LUKE 21:24

The "times of the Gentiles" reflects a biblical era characterized by Gentile domination, especially concerning Jerusalem. This era began with the Babylonian conquest of the city and the subsequent exile of its Jewish inhabitants. Throughout history, various Gentile empires have controlled Jerusalem—from the Babylonians to the Persians, Greeks, Romans, Byzantines, Arabs, Crusaders, Ottomans, and the British—until the city's partial return to Jewish hands in 1948 and its complete unification in 1967.

Jerusalem's reunification in 1967 was momentous. When the Israel Defense Forces (IDF) reclaimed the city, Colonel Motta Gur immediately broadcast the news over the army wireless: "The Temple Mount is in our hands!" The world watched in awe as young IDF soldiers wept while touching the Western Wall for the first time in their lives. Gur's announcement meant more than a military victory for the Jewish people; it carried the weight of a historical and spiritual homecoming. The city that had been their spiritual heart was once again in Jewish hands.[2]

However, despite the emotional and spiritual significance of this reunification, complexities persist. Even though Jerusalem is under Israeli sovereignty, the Temple Mount's management remains with the Islamic Waqf.[3] This paradox shows that spiritual authority remains divided while the city's political control has shifted.

The words of Jesus in Luke 21:24 foresaw a time when the Gentiles would trample Jerusalem until their allotted time was completed. When Jesus spoke those words, Jerusalem was under Roman control. He foresaw the city's continued subjugation and its eventual liberation. Does this level of control signify that the "times of the Gentiles" are not fully complete? Or is the political reunification of the city, coupled with Israel's rebirth, evidence enough?

The 1967 reunification was undeniably pivotal. After nearly twenty-five hundred years, Jerusalem was once again under Jewish sovereignty. This wasn't just a political transition but a monumental historical and prophetic milestone. The continuous

Gentile control, which began with Babylon's Nebuchadnezzar, was interrupted, signifying a shift in the prophetic timeline.

THE INGATHERING OF RUSSIAN JEWS (1970)

The prophecy:

> "Therefore, behold, the days are coming," says the LORD, "that they shall no longer say, 'As the LORD lives who brought up the children of Israel from the land of Egypt,' but, 'As the LORD lives who brought up and led the descendants of the house of Israel from the north country and from all the countries where I had driven them.' And they shall dwell in their own land."
>
> —JEREMIAH 23:7–8

In the 1970s, a significant wave of Soviet Jews, facing discrimination and persecution in the Soviet Union, began to immigrate to Israel. This movement marked the fulfillment of Jeremiah's (and others') promises that the descendants of Israel would be brought back.

It was a critical decade in the history of Soviet Jewry. The treatment of Jews in the Soviet Union had long been a cause of international concern. Anti-Semitism, state-sanctioned discrimination, and the suppression of religious freedom were daily realities for Jews living under Soviet rule. This led to widespread calls from the international community for the Soviet Union to allow its Jewish population the freedom to emigrate, and the international pressure intensified significantly during the Cold War era.

Western nations, particularly the United States, used diplomatic channels, public advocacy, and legislative actions to press for Soviet Jewish emigration. The issue became a key point of contention in the broader context of human rights during the Cold War. The US adoption of the Jackson-Vanik amendment in 1974 tied trade concessions to the USSR's willingness to allow emigration. While not exclusively focused on Jewish emigration, it was largely motivated by the plight of Soviet Jews and was a significant component of the international pressure campaign.

Simultaneously, grassroots movements advocating for Soviet Jews' rights were gaining traction. Activists organized demonstrations, disseminated information about the conditions faced by Soviet Jews, and lobbied politicians to act. This public advocacy played a crucial role in maintaining international attention and pressure on the issue.

In response to the mounting international pressure and changing internal dynamics, the Soviet Union began allowing increased numbers of Jews to emigrate. The 1970s saw significant emigration waves, with many Soviet Jews choosing to immigrate to Israel. The ability to escape anti-Semitism and oppression to freely practice their religion represented a significant victory for Soviet Jews and the international campaign advocating for their rights.

THE INGATHERING OF ETHIOPIAN JEWS (1984)

The prophecy:

> For then I will restore to the peoples a pure language, that they all may call on the name of the LORD, to serve Him with one accord. From beyond the rivers of Ethiopia My worshipers, the daughter of My dispersed ones, shall bring My offering.
>
> —ZEPHANIAH 3:9–10

Operations Moses, Joshua, and Solomon were a series of covert plans undertaken by the Israeli government and several international agencies in the 1980s and 1990s. Fulfilling the prophecy of Zephaniah 3:9–10, these operations were designed to rescue thousands of Ethiopian Jews, known as Beta Israel, who were trapped in the throes of civil war, famine, and religious persecution in Ethiopia and Sudan.

Operation Moses, the first of these missions, unfolded over seven weeks between 1984 and 1985. Involving secret airlifts from Sudanese refugee camps, the operation succeeded in transporting about 8,000 Ethiopian Jews to Israel. It was followed by Operation Joshua (also known as Operation Sheba) in 1985, which airlifted an additional 800 Ethiopian Jews to Israel. Finally, Operation Solomon, carried out in 1991, was a two-day, nonstop airlift that brought a staggering 14,325 Ethiopian Jews to Israel. The operation was of unprecedented scale and complexity involving the use of thirty-four Israeli aircraft.

The successful execution of these operations testified to the strength of global Jewish solidarity and Israel's commitment to the "ingathering of the exiles," a fundamental principle underlying the establishment of the State of Israel. The three operations led to a significant increase in the Ethiopian Jewish population in Israel.

The fact that the prophecy spoke specifically of a location "beyond the rivers of Ethiopia…" resonates deeply with the experiences of the Ethiopian Jews. Their journey from a region beyond the rivers of Ethiopia to their spiritual and ancestral home in Israel echoes the trials, perseverance, and ultimate redemption depicted in the prophecy.

The prophecy's reference to restoring a "pure language" indicates the restoration of Hebrew, the language of the Bible, among the Jews. Further, it signals a spiritual reunification, with the people serving the Lord "with one accord" in their ancestral homeland.

In summary, the successful execution of Operations Moses, Joshua, and Solomon underscores the remarkable endurance of the Jewish people and the power of prophetic fulfillment. Their journey "from beyond the rivers of Ethiopia" serves as a vivid testament to the survival and triumph of faith against formidable odds and the unfolding realization of the biblical vision of the return to Zion.

AMERICA WITHOUT GOD (SEPTEMBER 11, 2001)

The prophecy:

> He makes nations great, and destroys them; He enlarges nations, and guides them. He takes away the understanding of the chiefs of the people of the earth, and makes them wander in a pathless wilderness. They grope in the dark without light, and He makes them stagger like a drunken man.
>
> —JOB 12:23–25

September 11, 2001, will always be remembered by anyone connected with the attacks on America on that day. But placed in a historic context, the date carries a profound sense of divine mystery and significance. It is as if events, separated by time, were intricately woven together, pointing to a higher purpose and a greater narrative unfolding over time.

In 1609, September 11 was the day Henry Hudson sailed into New York Bay on his ship, the *Half Moon,* during his search for a Northwest passage to the Far East. This momentous voyage set in motion a series of events that would shape the destiny of the city as a global financial center.

Fast forward to September 11, 1941. On that day, President Franklin D. Roosevelt delivered a pivotal speech that laid the groundwork for America's rise as a global economic and military superpower. That same day, construction began on the Pentagon.

Of course, September 11, 2001, is now known as "9/11"—the day of coordinated terrorist attacks on the World Trade Center, a symbol of America's economic prowess, and the Pentagon, representing its military might. The haunting and tragic results of that attack shook the nation and the world to its core.

Ironically, on September 11, 2001, a replica of Henry Hudson's ship, the *Half Moon*, went sailing past the crumbling towers in New York, adding to the enigmatic nature of the date.[4] It is as if history came full circle, linking the exploratory spirit of the past with the enduring resilience of the present. It reminds us that prosperity and security come from God—and disobedience and rebellion can lead to His withdrawal of favor and protection.

As Job's words remind us, God will not be mocked.

THE GREAT FALLING AWAY (2020)

The prophecy:

> Let no one deceive you by any means; for that Day will not come unless the falling away comes first, and the man of sin is revealed, the son of perdition, who opposes and exalts himself above all that is called God or that is worshiped, so that he sits as God in the temple of God, showing himself that he is God.
>
> —2 THESSALONIANS 2:3–4

The "great falling away" is often understood as a significant apostasy or departure from the faith—a spiritual erosion that will occur before the second coming of Jesus Christ. It is seen as a time when many individuals who once professed to be followers of Christ will abandon their faith or turn away from the truth of the gospel. This turning away is thought to be a widespread and global phenomenon, marking a period of spiritual decline and moral decay.

The concept comes from various New Testament revelations, specifically the one from 2 Thessalonians 2:3–4. Before the

Antichrist is revealed, society will undergo a great falling away from the faith. We can expect many people who are professing Christians to embrace lies and doctrines of demons. This falling away will not be immediate; it will be a progressive decline. Additional information is provided in 2 Timothy 3:1–5:

> But know this, that in the last days perilous times will come: For men will be lovers of themselves, lovers of money, boasters, proud, blasphemers, disobedient to parents, unthankful, unholy, unloving, unforgiving, slanderers, without self-control, brutal, despisers of good, traitors, headstrong, haughty, lovers of pleasure rather than lovers of God, having a form of godliness but denying its power.

The year 2020 presented numerous challenges and uncertainties that contributed significantly to a great falling away from the Christian faith. The COVID-19 pandemic had far-reaching effects on individuals, communities, and societies worldwide, influencing people's perspectives, priorities, and beliefs. The enemy used this crisis to take advantage of people's struggles and caused many to question their faith or become disillusioned.

THE RED HEIFER APPEARS (2022)

The prophecy:

> Now the LORD spoke to Moses and Aaron, saying, "This is the ordinance of the law which the LORD has commanded, saying: 'Speak to the children of Israel, that they bring you a red heifer without blemish, in which there is no defect and on which a yoke has never come. You shall give it to Eleazar the priest, that he may take it outside the camp, and it shall be slaughtered before him....Then a man who is clean shall gather up the ashes of the heifer, and store them outside the camp in a clean place; and they shall be kept for the

congregation of the children of Israel for the water of purification; it is for purifying from sin."

—Numbers 19:1–3, 9

The red heifer holds a unique role in Jewish tradition. Its significance lies in its rarity and the specific requirements for it to be considered suitable for the purification process. According to Jewish law, the red heifer must be without blemish, free from any defects, and have never borne a yoke. These stringent criteria, coupled with the natural rarity of red heifers, makes their appearance a truly extraordinary event.

For centuries, the search for a red heifer that meets the biblical requirements has been a matter of great interest and speculation among religious scholars. Historically, there have been a few instances where individuals or groups claimed to have found a suitable red heifer, but thorough examination ultimately revealed that they did not meet the criteria.

In 2022, however, *five* red heifers were reported to have been found that met the requirements outlined in Numbers 19. This discovery sent shockwaves through religious communities and sparked intense discussions among theologians, biblical scholars, and believers. The red heifers are currently in a secure, undisclosed location in Israel. They are now two years old and (according to Jewish rabbinic guidelines) need to be at least three years old to meet the requirements, which would be in 2024. This is a wonderful reminder that we are on a very precise prophetic timeline for the rituals involving the red heifer and the reconstruction of the third temple, which is a major step toward the fulfillment of end-times events.

THE DAYS OF ELIJAH

The prophecy:

> Behold, I will send you Elijah the prophet before the coming
> of the great and dreadful day of the LORD. And he will turn
> the hearts of the fathers to the children, and the hearts of
> the children to their fathers, lest I come and strike the earth
> with a curse.
>
> —MALACHI 4:5–6

The "days of Elijah" is a concept that holds deep significance in end-times prophecy. The spirit of Elijah, as described in the prophecy, is believed to manifest in a unique way, leading up to the second coming of Jesus Christ. It is associated with an unprecedented measure of God's power and prophetic revelation, a transformative period of spiritual awakening and righteousness.

Broken Families: One significant sign associated with the days of Elijah is a reversal of the breakdown of traditional family structures and the increase in broken families. The deterioration of family units is a consequence of broader spiritual decline, leading to various societal challenges. This prophetic promise underscores the importance of family values and the need for spiritual and emotional healing within households: the mending of broken relationships to restore the bonds between parents and children.

Renewed Spiritual Power Among Men: The days of Elijah prophecy also points to the restoration of spiritual power among men. This is a call to spiritual leadership and responsibility within the family, community, and religious associations. The fulfillment of this aspect of the prophecy will empower men to take on active roles as spiritual leaders and protectors, promoting righteousness and moral integrity.

Reuniting of Fathers and Sons: Central to the prophecy of the days of Elijah is the theme of reconciliation and reunion between fathers and sons.

The Clock Is Ticking

The concept of a prophetic clock in relation to end-time events in the Bible points to the belief that certain prophecies and signs serve as markers of the approaching fulfillment of God's plan for the end of the age. The events on the clock signal the progression of God's divine plan and remind us to remain vigilant.

While many prophecies have already been fulfilled, crucial events are still to come. The rebuilding of the temple in Jerusalem, the rapture when believers are taken up to be with Christ, the tribulation period, and the second coming of Jesus Christ are yet to be realized.

As we navigate the uncertainties of the future, it is essential to maintain a posture of faith, hope, and watchfulness. The prophetic clock reminds us that God's timing is perfect. His promises will be fulfilled in due course. In the meantime we are to stay rooted in our faith, living lives of righteousness and compassion while eagerly anticipating the fulfillment of God's final plans for the world.

Amid the prophetic clock's ticking, our responsibility as believers is to share the message of salvation and hope with the world, inviting others to find refuge in the love and grace of Jesus Christ. As we eagerly await the culmination of these prophetic events, let us stand firm in our faith, trusting in the sovereign hand of God and the assurance that His purposes will ultimately prevail. May we be faithful stewards of the time we have been given, striving to bring light to a world in need of hope, peace, and redemption.

Part II: A Look Ahead

SOME PROPHECIES IN Scripture are apocalyptic, symbolic, and often more than a little confusing. Many people tend to discount those as being irresolvable. Other prophetic statements are quite clear and understandable, yet the events they predict may appear to be too frightening, too bizarre, or too good to be true, so they too are ignored.

But biblical prophecy is there for a reason. It was included in sacred Scripture for our benefit. Even if we "just don't get it" right away, that's no reason to dismiss what God's prophets have foretold. Several of Jesus' parables require repeated reading and much pondering before we make sense of what Jesus was saying, yet we keep working to comprehend their meaning. The same should be true of prophecy.

In this section, we'll look at a few of the specific events we're told to expect at the midnight hour. We'll also see how many of these things we expect to happen "someday" may already be much closer than many people realize. And with a little effort, a better understanding of biblical prophecy can even help explain much of the confusion and chaos taking place in our world today.

Chapter 4

Sequence of Events to Come

Y OU'VE PROBABLY SEEN the "COEXIST" bumper sticker. If not, the word is expressed with each letter designed to represent a different belief system. (For example, the C is a crescent moon with star, the X is a star of David, the T is a cross.) At first glance, it might seem to present a positive message. If you take it as a reminder that we are a pluralistic society that should respect all people and their beliefs, that's a noble sentiment. However, if it is perceived as a subtle suggestion that all religions, when stood side by side, carry the same weight and importance, then the sentiment is not so noble. If that's the message people come away with, then it implies that Jesus was wrong when He said, "I am the way, the truth, and the life. No one comes to the Father except through Me" (John 14:6).

Many in the church became quite upset in 1971 when John Lennon released "Imagine," his song promoting a society with no heaven, no hell, no countries, "and no religion too." Believers were rankled at the thought of a world with no religion, yet many hardly blink twice at a culture so tolerant that all religions are treated equally. They count it a victory if Buddhists, Hindus, Muslims, and others acknowledge that Jesus was a wise and influential teacher. But since Jesus claimed to be God, to concede that He was only a good teacher means little.

C. S. Lewis said we have only three possible responses to Jesus' claims to be God:

> I am trying here to prevent anyone saying the really foolish thing that people often say about Him: "I'm ready to accept Jesus as a great moral teacher, but I don't accept His claim to be God." That is the one thing we must not say. A man who was merely a man and said the sort of things Jesus said would not be a great moral teacher. He would either be a lunatic—on a level with the man who says he is a poached egg—or else he would be the Devil of Hell. You must make your choice. Either this man was, and is, the Son of God: or else a madman or something worse. You can shut Him up for a fool, you can spit at Him and kill Him as a demon; or you can fall at His feet and call Him Lord and God. But let us not come with any patronising nonsense about His being a great human teacher. He has not left that open to us. He did not intend to.[1]

So Jesus was either who He said He was—the Lord—or He was a liar or a lunatic. But we shouldn't be surprised to see widespread, conscientious attempts to synchronize all religions into a single global belief system. Such efforts are only one item on an increasingly outspoken agenda to formulate a one-world government.

MOVING TOWARD A ONE-WORLD GOVERNMENT

Now, before you accuse me of jumping onto the latest conspiracy theory, let me remind you that end-times prophecy describes the existence of many nations that will all fall under the leadership of a single individual who dictates even the ability to buy and sell. Several years ago I wrote about the increasing spread of lawlessness in our nation and specifically about "the lawless one" (the Antichrist) who will come.[2] Since then I've been seeing more and more events that seem to be preparing the way for such a world leader.

The aim of a one-world government is a borderless world. We're seeing borders being weakened with increasing numbers of border crossings. Even with the implementation of new immigration policies intended to limit the numbers of people pouring into the United States from the south, fewer who make it here are being sent back.[3]

Other countries have much worse problems with massive influxes of refugees. The civil war in Syria accounts for over 25 percent of the global refugee population. The war in Ukraine forced millions to leave their homes. Severe humanitarian crises in Venezuela prompted 5.6 million citizens to flee and seek asylum in neighboring countries. Several countries in Africa are similarly affected by local wars, ethnic discrimination and violence, the COVID-19 pandemic, food insecurity, and more.

The problem adds up to the fact that, on a global level, the number of refugees and internally displaced people increased from 82.4 million people at the end of 2020 to over 103 million by mid-2022. One in every 78 people in the world is now forcibly displaced—and more than 36 million of them are children.[4] Border lines are becoming less concrete.

The language of gender is another element in the recent trend toward conformity and "oneness"—an attempt to remove anything that makes someone different or unique and instead seeks conformity on every level. For years now, English-speaking people have been urged to adopt more (often awkward) gender-inclusive language. Publishing and print style manuals have been updated to dictate what language is appropriate to keep from offending someone by using "he" or "she." The same changes are being made in many other languages, including Spanish, French, Swedish, Arabic, Hebrew, and more.[5]

This doesn't sound at all like a conspiracy theory to me. When we see such great numbers of people who are desperate to find someone who will hear them, protect them, care for them, and offer some glimmer of hope for their future, doesn't that sound like just the opportunity for a charismatic leader to arise with promises to resolve their problems if only everyone will unite under his authority?

The Bible was written by inspiration of God to inform us, to make us ready and equip us for the things that are coming in our lifetime. It is the living Word of God, inspired by God. It will never fail. It will do everything it says; it is inerrant. It tells us what's going to happen yet doesn't include a step-by-step plan for how the world is going to get there. Instead, Jesus instructs us to "Take heed, watch and pray; for you do not know when the time is" (Mark 13:33). Similarly, the apostle Paul challenges us to "Watch, stand fast in the faith, be brave, be strong" (1 Cor. 16:13). Jesus chided those who "know how to discern the face of the sky, but you cannot discern the signs of the times" (Matt. 16:3).

So let's look at some signs we ought to be watching for, beginning with this idea that a globalist agenda exists with the aim of bringing all people under the control of a one-world government, with a few powerful people in charge. Globalism is developing in opposition to nationalism, which is getting a lot of bad press right now.

Nationalism promotes the interests of a nation, especially sovereignty over its homeland. America is a sovereign nation—one nation, under God—with a proud history and a long-established system of self-government. We acknowledge the right of other nations to govern themselves as well. However, lately we have seen an antinationalism movement in the United States, and it's very strategic.

Efforts are being made to not only question our rich history as a nation but to rewrite it. It's as if all that matters to many people is what's taking place now. They treat the past as if once something is done, it can be ignored and then quickly forgotten. This trend is manifest in actions like pulling down a statue. Why not? That was then and this is now, so all that's important is today. Yet if you evaluate everything based only on today, you lose track of not only what you did right but also what you did wrong. And if you remove the favor of God on our nation from our history, we then become like other nations—which seems to be the point.

You see evidence of this antinationalism in sports—with individuals, or perhaps entire teams, disrespecting the national anthem before a game. One basketball team owner even refused to play the anthem before his team's games until the leadership of the NBA forced him to. But I think such actions reflect the heart of what's happening in these global elites.

We are unique among all the nations of the world in that God has blessed us with a favor beyond measure. Our country was founded upon godly principles. And while we may not have lived up to our stated beliefs at times, until recently we've always believed "In God we trust." Yet years ago the global agenda moved from the political arena into the religious. In the 1960s we saw legal action to remove the Pledge of Allegiance from schools, to discontinue prayer and reading the Bible, and to take the Ten Commandments off the walls. So this is not new. This global agenda has been going on for some time.

The Great Falling Away

I believe all these shifts in public thinking are indicators that we are fast approaching (or have already begun) what Scripture refers to as "the falling away." Here's the context from 2 Thessalonians 2, a pivotal chapter in understanding the last days:

> Now, brethren, concerning the coming of our Lord Jesus Christ and our gathering together to Him, we ask you, not to be soon shaken in mind or troubled, either by spirit or by word or by letter, as if from us, as though the day of Christ had come. Let no one deceive you by any means; for that Day will not come unless the falling away comes first, and the man of sin is revealed, the son of perdition, who opposes and exalts himself above all that is called God or that is worshiped, so that he sits as God in the temple of God, showing himself that he is God.
>
> —2 Thessalonians 2:1–4

You should recall the "Great Falling Away" from the prophetic clock in the previous chapter, but we'll go into more detail here. Scripture says that as we approach the last days, we can expect to see more and more people falling away from the faith. Many who claim to be Christians and love God will deny Him and withdraw from all kingdom activity.

I believe this falling away has already begun and that the recent season of COVID-19 became a turning point prophetically. I heard a lot of people saying, "I really don't think I need church anymore." For some people, COVID was just the excuse they were looking for to detach from what had become little more than a spiritual routine. They were coasting, and when their church went virtual, it was easy to simply drift away. Others had better intentions but similar results. They continued to get up every weekend, watch a streamed church service from the comfort of their sofas—perhaps still in pajamas—and then go about their day. But after a couple of months, it wasn't every weekend. And the music just wasn't the same when it wasn't live. And the neighbors mowing their lawns and splashing in their pools were distractions during the message. And eventually they stopped making any effort at all. Although their "falling away" took longer, it was just as real, and it was just as much a loss to the kingdom.

In April 2020, shortly after the COVID restrictions were imposed, I was in a gathering of about three hundred pastors where all of us were trying to figure out how to respond. Most of us decided to reopen on May 31. The consensus was that we didn't want to keep our church doors closed any longer than necessary. And since May 31 was also Pentecost Sunday, we felt that day was an appropriate time to ask for the movement of the Spirit of God in our churches.

But not everyone was on board. I talked to a couple of young pastors at the gathering who had recently started a church. They told me, "Everything's working so well online that we're never going to go back live, even after they lift the restrictions." I asked them why not, and they said, "Well, we found that we're just as effective. People are still giving. So why would we go through all the trouble?" When pastors of churches find that it's too much trouble to open their doors to the people of their community, that's a falling away.

Some of you reading this might suggest I'm being judgmental. After all, didn't Jesus say, "Judge not, that you be not judged"? (Matt. 7:1). Yes, but a few verses later He also said, "Beware of false prophets....A good tree cannot bear bad fruit, nor can a bad tree bear good fruit. Every tree that does not bear good fruit is cut down and thrown into the fire. Therefore by their fruits you will know them" (Matt. 7:15, 18-20). And adding to that concern, John wrote in his first letter:

> Little children, it is the last hour; and as you have heard that the Antichrist is coming, even now many antichrists have come, by which we know that it is the last hour. They went out from us, but they were not of us; for if they had been of us, they would have continued with us; but they went out that they might be made manifest, that none of them were of us.
>
> —1 John 2:18-19

Believers are challenged not to judge one another, yet to also keep our eyes open to leaders who might mislead us, whether intentionally or not. We aren't being judgmental when we attempt to discern between someone who is speaking God's truth and someone who is promoting a practice or doctrine against the clear teaching of Scripture.

We need to get better at that. In fact, I believe the recent great falling away is due largely to excessive tolerance of sin among believers. No one likes to be called judgmental. We (rightly) want to be considered loving, compassionate, tolerant, and Christlike, yet when dealing with someone embroiled in blatant sin with no indication of ever changing, tolerance is not the answer. We are called to not only "walk as children of light," but also to "have no fellowship with the unfruitful works of darkness, but rather *expose* them" (Eph. 5:8, 11, emphasis added). The church is called to excise sin from the body and continue to grow spiritually. Those who don't risk falling away.

The Departure of God's Spirit

Why is this so important? Because while the great falling away is bad enough in itself, we saw from 2 Thessalonians that it is a precursor to something even worse: the rise of the "man of sin"—the Antichrist. Still, wouldn't the church be enough of an influence to combat such an event? This is explained a little further down in 2 Thessalonians 2:

For the mystery of lawlessness is already at work; only He who now restrains will do so until He is taken out of the way. And then the lawless one will be revealed, whom the Lord will consume with the breath of His mouth and destroy with the brightness of His coming. The coming of the lawless one is according to the working of Satan, with all power, signs, and lying wonders, and with all unrighteous deception among those who perish, because they did not receive the love of the truth, that they might be saved. And for this reason God will send them strong delusion, that they should believe the lie, that they all may be condemned who did not believe the truth but had pleasure in unrighteousness.

—2 THESSALONIANS 2:7–12

Paul tells us in this passage that the Holy Spirit is "He who now restrains" the power of evil in the world. But when the time is right, the Holy Spirit will withdraw to allow people to run their lives the way they want to.

Do you realize that the only hope on planet Earth right now is the church of the living God empowered by the Spirit of God? But imagine if the Spirit were no longer here to restrain the rampant wickedness. Envision schools with no Christian students and teachers trying to make a positive difference. No Christian legislators trying to enact and enforce good and moral laws. No more power in the churches to oppose the increasing number of evildoers.

This was essentially what happened just prior to the great flood. "The LORD said, 'My Spirit shall not strive with man forever, for he is indeed flesh'" (Gen. 6:3). If we continually resist the leading of the Spirit of God, He will step back and let us run life our way. And isn't it interesting that Jesus said if we want to know about His return, study the days of Noah and the days of Lot (Luke 17:26–30)? (More on that in chapter 8.)

So 2 Thessalonians 2 tells us to expect a falling away, followed by the withdrawal of the Holy Spirit, allowing a rise to power of the Antichrist, who will organize and head a lockstep march to globalism and one-world government. Don't expect this transition of allegiances to occur instantly. Such changes happen progressively, don't they? A falling away from God is usually gradual; it rarely happens overnight. For a while you're regularly putting in time and effort to grow in your faith, and then you relax your efforts just a bit—and then a little more. The difference is hardly noticeable. The slide is ever so gradual until one day you hit bottom and wonder how you got there.

SETTING THE STAGE FOR THE ANTICHRIST

When God's Spirit withdraws, this falling away will intensify and affect great numbers of people, allowing the emergence of a malevolent world leader. What does this leader want? Above all, he wants *control*. How does someone gain control over large numbers of people? It starts with knowing who his subjects are and what they are doing.

Two *New York Times* writers recently proved it isn't that hard to do. In 2019, a source gave them a digital file with the precise locations of more than twelve million smartphones for several months in 2016 and 2017. The data had been collected by smartphone apps and filtered through software used for digital advertising. The data was supposed to be anonymous, but it took very little effort on the writers' part to identify "celebrities, Pentagon officials and average Americans." They write, "It became clear that this data...was a liability to national security, to free assembly and to citizens leading mundane lives. It provided an intimate record of people whether they were visiting drug treatment centers, strip clubs, casinos, abortion clinics or places of worship."[6]

A year later, they received another collection of data—about 100,000 location pings from thousands of smartphones of Donald Trump's supporters. They were not only able to identify around 130 devices inside the Capitol when it was being stormed but could also track those who moved from the Trump rally at the National Mall to the Capitol and could even trace phones to and from many of their homes, even those in Florida, Kentucky, South Carolina, New Mexico, and elsewhere. The *Times* reporters explain:

> This new data included a remarkable piece of information: a unique ID for each user that is tied to a smartphone. This made it even easier to find people, since the supposedly anonymous ID could be matched with other databases containing the same ID, allowing us to add real names, addresses, phone numbers, email addresses and other information about smartphone owners in seconds....Our findings show the promise of anonymity is a farce. Several companies offer tools to allow anyone with data to match the IDs with other databases....There are no laws forcing companies to disclose what the data is used for or for how long. There are no legal requirements to ever delete the data....Their movements could be bought and sold to innumerable parties for years. [7]

Plenty of Americans remain oblivious to this collection of data through no fault of their own, but many others who understand what's happening allow it anyway. They feel powerless to stop it, or they're simply willing to sacrifice their privacy for the convenience provided by smartphones. The dark truth is that despite genuine concern from those paying attention, there's little appetite for a meaningful dismantling of this advertising infrastructure that undergirds unchecked corporate data collection. Like it or not, this is one method—already in use—of allowing unknown entities a certain level of control over us. In the hands of a truly sinister figure, much of the information we willingly provide could be used against us.

Another means of control is through business. A one-world government would require a standard economic model. Already a movement is underway to replace capitalism. Every ideology has its problems and critics, of course, and capitalism is no exception. Yet capitalism is the reason our nation has prospered. The belief that "If I work hard, I might just get ahead" has inspired people to do just that, resulting in freedom and prosperity—not just for the large corporations, but for the thousands of mom-and-pop businesses across the country.

Yes, some companies get greedy and prioritize short-term profits over long-term commitments to their employees. The perspective of Klaus Schwab, founder and executive chairman of the World Economic Forum, is that "the same economic system that created so much prosperity in the golden age of American capitalism in the 1950s and 1960s is now creating inequality and climate change. And the same political system that enabled our global progress and democracy after World War II now contributes to societal discord and discontent. Each was well intended but had unintended negative consequences."[8]

What's his solution? It's called the "Great Reset." Plans have been underway for several years, but the 2020 COVID-19 pandemic appears to have been the catalyst to move forward. With its initial economic downturn and concerns about creating the worst depression since the 1930s, this was their proposed solution. Again, Klaus Schwab speaks for the World Economic Forum: "To achieve a better outcome, the world must act jointly and swiftly to revamp all aspects of our societies and economies, from education to social contracts and working conditions. Every country, from the United States to China, must participate, and every industry, from oil and gas to tech, must be transformed. In short, we need a 'Great Reset' of capitalism."[9]

Instead of traditional capitalism, this high-profile group proposes that the world should adopt more socialistic policies such as wealth taxes, additional regulations, and massive "green" urban infrastructure programs. The stated goals of this great reset are noble: reforms of businesses harmful to the environment, more income equality and sustainability, and support of the public good, among others, yet this new proposed worldwide structure doesn't appear to bode well if you're a small business owner.

We know from reading Revelation that in addition to other kinds of control being imposed, one will be a change of currency. When the Antichrist comes to power, he will require a physical mark on anyone who wishes to do business: "He causes all, both small and great, rich and poor, free and slave, to receive a mark on their right hand or on their foreheads, and that no one may buy or sell except one who has the mark or the name of the beast, or the number of his name" (Rev. 13:16–17).

Let's talk a little bit about digital currency, or cryptocurrency. What's the problem with cash? When I go to pay for something at Ace Hardware, the first thing they ask is, "Would you like to give me your phone number?" I say, "No, I'd like to give you cash," but it's getting to the point where they don't know what to do with cash anymore. It's disturbing enough that fewer clerks seem capable of counting out change without the help of the cash register, but a much bigger concern is that cryptocurrency tracks and controls every dollar. That means it's possible for the government to determine where you've been, what you've done, and what you spent your money on. Why does that matter? Well, it might be very appealing to the IRS, for example, because you can't hide any money. Grandma can't roll up a couple of hundreds and put them in a sock drawer or hide them in her closet. If I pay cash for something, that transaction is my business alone. But if cash is eliminated, so is much personal privacy and/or freedom.

I don't know why I can't look for a couch online without it showing up in my Facebook feed. I may not want everyone to know I'm looking for a couch. I might want to keep my couch preferences private. But no. That's now the world we're living in, and it's likely to get worse.

In 2014 China introduced what they call a social credit system, and they've been developing it since then. It is "a moral ranking system…that will monitor the behavior of its enormous population—and rank them all based on their 'social credit.'" It will apply to companies and government organizations as well as individuals. "The plan is for the social credit system to eventually be mandatory and unified across the nation, with each person given their own unique code used to measure their social credit score in real-time."[10]

Scores can go up or down, dependent on behavior. They can drop due to smoking in nonsmoking areas, posting fake news online, fraud, bad driving, unpaid debts, and other offenses. Offenders can be punished for low scores by being banned from flights, denied enrollment at the better schools and universities, or placed on public blacklists that can prevent being hired or receiving contracts. Those with improving social credit are rewarded with better interest rates, ability to rent items or book hotels without a deposit, and discounts on energy bills.[11]

Imagine if your government ranked you based on what you've posted or said privately, or on your most recent purchases. Imagine if they, through a growing surveillance network of 200 million cameras, used facial recognition and other mechanical techniques to have eyes on you and your behavior twenty-four hours a day, seven days a week. Finally, imagine if the people in power distilled all that data down to a single metric to rank your trustworthiness as a citizen. Well, it's real and it's already happening. Someone has called China's social credit system "a futuristic vision of Big Brother out of control."[12] If we're not there already, that's the direction we seem to be heading.

ANY *GOOD* NEWS?

The way the present day is shaping up can look rather grim. And when we see the biblical forecast of things yet to come—which appear to be rapidly approaching—it looks even worse. But let me assure you, knowledge of what the Word of God says and awareness of what's happening in your world is never a bad thing. We do ourselves an immense disservice if we focus solely on the gloom and doom of a fearful future without balancing that scenario with an even greater reality: the presence and power of God. Let me suggest a couple of scriptures to remind us of those two things.

One of my favorites is Psalm 91, which I recommend committing to memory or at least putting on your refrigerator. It begins: "He who dwells in the secret place of the Most High shall abide under the shadow of the Almighty. I will say of the LORD, 'He is my refuge and my fortress; My God, in Him I will trust.' Surely He shall deliver you from the snare of the fowler and from the perilous pestilence. He shall cover you with His feathers, and under His wings you shall take refuge" (Ps. 91:1–4). The psalm goes on from there with additional assurances of God's presence and protection.

Did you know that God has a secret place? Let that sink in for a minute. You may have a secret place where you go to pray or be all alone. God also has a secret place where He invites us not only to visit but to *dwell*. Why should we ever be intimidated by those who think they are high in society when we reside with the Most High? Why should we fear powerful people when we abide under the shadow of our almighty God?

A similar sentiment is expressed in Romans 8:

> Who shall separate us from the love of Christ? Shall tribulation, or distress, or persecution, or famine, or nakedness, or peril, or sword? As it is written: "For Your sake we are killed all day long; we are accounted as sheep for the slaughter." Yet in all these things we are more than conquerors through Him who loved us. For I am persuaded that neither death nor life, nor angels nor principalities nor powers, nor things present nor things to come, nor height nor depth, nor any other created thing, shall be able to separate us from the love of God which is in Christ Jesus our Lord.
>
> —Romans 8:35–39

God's people are constantly under His protection. The Bible is replete with references to those whom God has delivered from the snare and the perilous pestilence. So when we see our own uncertain circumstances in life, why are we so prone to give up? We need to take our eyes off the problem and direct them back toward God.

Perseverance is a command of God. Don't quit. Don't give up. And don't worry: "Be anxious for nothing, but in everything by prayer and supplication, with thanksgiving, let your requests be made known to God; and the peace of God, which surpasses all understanding, will guard your hearts and minds through Christ Jesus" (Phil. 4:6–7).

Here's the good news: regardless of your painful circumstances—even if they are trials brought on by the approach of the last days—you can count on the power and presence of God to see you through them. And when those trials are finally over, God's people will still be standing strong for all eternity.

Chapter 5

Rise of the Antichrist

I N 1948, FRANK Wisner's appointment as director of the
Office of Special Projects (OSP) marked a significant turning
point in the history of the United States' intelligence commu-
nity. The OSP, soon renamed the Office of Policy Coordination
(OPC), was created as a covert branch of the Central Intelligence
Agency (CIA). Its primary goal was to engage in espionage and
counterintelligence activities abroad to combat the spread of
Communism during the early days of the Cold War.[1]

However, Wisner saw an opportunity to extend the reach of
the agency's influence beyond foreign borders. He recognized the
power of media and the potential to shape public opinion domestically and internationally. This realization led to the inception
of another covert program known as Operation Mockingbird.[2]

The central aim of Operation Mockingbird was to exert control
over the American media by influencing the narrative presented
to the public. The CIA sought to establish connections with journalists, editors, and media executives in influential news outlets.
Through such connections, they could manipulate news stories, plant disinformation, and promote certain political agendas
favorable to the government's interests. Over time, Operation

Mockingbird expanded its network of influence, gaining significant control over major media organizations. Notable newspapers such as *The New York Times, The Washington Post*, and the *New York Post*, as well as prominent news agencies such as CBS and *Time* magazine, came under its sway. These outlets, with their vast readership and viewership, became valuable tools in shaping public perception of critical issues, both domestic and international.

One of the key aspects of Operation Mockingbird was its ability to ensure that certain stories were given prominence while others were suppressed or downplayed. By strategically managing the dissemination of information, the CIA could control public opinion, steer debates, and protect national interests, often in ways unknown to the general population.

The program's influence wasn't limited to shaping news content. It also involved infiltrating entertainment and cultural spheres. Hollywood wasn't immune to Operation Mockingbird's manipulations. The CIA sought to influence the portrayal of certain themes and characters in movies and television shows, subtly promoting ideologies that aligned with the government's objectives.

As Operation Mockingbird continued to expand its reach, it faced growing criticism and skepticism. Concerns arose about the ethical implications of covertly controlling the media and undermining the principles of a free press. Journalists and media professionals were wary of potential interference in their work and the risk of compromising journalistic integrity.

Though the full extent of Operation Mockingbird's activities remains unclear due to its covert nature, subsequent investigations and reports shed light on the program's existence and raised questions about its long-term impact on the media landscape.

THE MASTER MANIPULATOR

The proliferation of fake news in today's digital age plays a significant role in shaping public perception and preparing the groundwork for the rise of a manipulative and deceptive leader. The spread of false information and misinformation can create an environment of confusion and distrust, making people more susceptible and paving the way for the lies and deception of the Antichrist.

The idea of a one-world government is a controversial topic that has been discussed by various groups and individuals over the years. Some proponents argue that a unified global governance structure could promote peace, cooperation, and efficient management of global challenges. Critics of this concept express concerns about potential abuses of power, loss of national sovereignty, and challenges related to cultural and political diversity.

According to the Bible, the Antichrist will accomplish this goal of global domination. Here are some of the ways he might achieve this aim:

1. RISING TO POWER THROUGH DECEPTION

The Antichrist will emerge as charismatic and influential, deceiving the masses with false promises of peace, unity, and prosperity. Through skillful manipulation of public opinion and exploitation of people's insecurities and desires, he will gain a worldwide following. After the mysterious disappearance of true believers during the rapture, fear and uncertainty will prevail. Desperate for security and stability, people will be willing to give up everything, even their very souls, in pursuit of the utopia he promises. As the world grapples with confusion and turmoil, the Antichrist will seize this moment of vulnerability, skillfully wielding the power of deception to captivate hearts and minds. The longing for security and answers will make the masses susceptible to his deceitful tactics.

The term *Christ* ("anointed one") is the Greek equivalent for the Hebrew *Messiah*. The title holds significant weight in the Bible, representing God's promised deliverer and leader. Throughout history, many have claimed to be prophets and messiahs. The Antichrist will follow in their footsteps, finding tremendous success that none of the previous deceivers came close to achieving. Amidst the chaos, the Antichrist's true nature will remain veiled from the world for a time. But behind the facade of peace and unity will lurk a malevolent ambition, seeking to control and enslave humanity. As his power increases, others' devotion to him will no longer be optional; it will be under threat of death.

However, some will discern the darkness behind the charismatic charm, holding onto the light of truth, determined not to be swayed by false promises. During this tumultuous time, echoes of Jesus' warning will resound, urging the faithful not to be deceived by charismatic leaders who claim to be the Messiah: "Then if anyone says to you, 'Look, here is the Christ!' or, 'Look, He is there!' do not believe it. For false christs and false prophets will rise and show signs and wonders to deceive, if possible, even the elect. But take heed; see, I have told you all things beforehand" (Mark 13:21-23).

The last days will be a time of testing for all mankind. The battle between truth and deception will rage on in an epic clash that transcends mortal struggles. As the demons of hell are released to work an evil plan, the Antichrist's rise to power through deception will set the stage for the battle of Armageddon.

2. Exploiting Global Crises

The Antichrist may take advantage of worldwide crises (wars, economic instability, natural disasters, climate change, and others) to present himself as a savior who will solve these problems. The concept of leaders using a crisis to gain or consolidate power is a proven strategy throughout history. In ancient Rome, the institution of dictatorship was a constitutional part of the republic's system. The Senate might appoint a dictator in times of emergency, such as war, and give him extraordinary powers to resolve the crisis. This position, however, was temporary, only meant to last until the crisis was averted.

But this mechanism, intended as a safeguard to protect the state in times of crisis, also had the potential to be abused. For example, Julius Caesar was appointed dictator during the civil wars of the late republic, and he eventually became *dictator perpetuo*, or "dictator in perpetuity." This move marked the end of the Roman Republic and the start of the Roman Empire.

The rise of Adolf Hitler to power in Germany was expedited by a combination of economic crisis, political instability, and exploitation of nationalistic sentiments, alongside Hitler's own political maneuvering and charismatic appeal. Hitler proposed the Enabling Act in 1933, which gave the chancellor the power to pass laws without the involvement of the Reichstag (German parliament). The act effectively transformed Hitler's government into a legal dictatorship.

We expect that the Antichrist will rise to power in a manner that makes sense in the context of some future crises. Daniel predicted as much. His prophecies warned that "Through his cunning he shall cause deceit to prosper under his rule" (Dan. 8:25), and "he shall come in peaceably, and seize the kingdom by intrigue" (Dan. 11:21).

3. ESTABLISHING A TOTALITARIAN REGIME

Once in power, the Antichrist will consolidate his authority through a totalitarian regime, suppressing dissent and eliminating opposition. This may involve utilizing advanced surveillance technologies and controlling information flow to maintain dominance.

George Orwell's novel *1984* envisioned a society under the constant surveillance of an authoritarian regime, represented by the figure of "Big Brother." The phrase "Big Brother is watching you" has since become symbolic of the invasive surveillance (from many sources) that continues to increase in both scope and intensity. The resulting deterioration of personal privacy has become our reality, given the advancement of technology since Orwell's time. Here are a few examples:

- *Pervasiveness of technology.* The arrival of smartphones, smart homes, and hundreds of other "smart" devices had widespread appeal for making our lives simpler and more efficient. Now, however, it has become a different story as our watches, appliances, fitness trackers, and all kinds of other devices collect data on us, and we don't know exactly what it's being used for.

- *Social media and online tracking.* Online activities, from searches to social interactions, can be tracked and analyzed. The accumulated data can be used to create detailed profiles of individuals' behaviors, interests, beliefs, and relationships.

- *Government surveillance of personal data.* Often justified as a measure for national security, the government keeps tabs on its citizens. It is often a necessary requirement for federal programs such as Social Security, Medicare, paying taxes, and so forth, but sometimes it's shocking to discover just how much data is being collected. For example, the Snowden revelations in 2013 exposed the extent of government surveillance programs in the United States and around the world.

- *Surveillance by private corporations.* Large tech companies, among others, collect vast amounts of data on their users. Although this information is gathered for targeted advertising, it could also be used for more invasive purposes or be accessed by other governments with nefarious intent.

- *AI and Big Data.* Advances in artificial intelligence and big data analysis now allow huge volumes of data to be processed and analyzed, almost instantly, in ways that can reveal detailed insights about individuals and groups.

- *Facial recognition and biometrics.* Technologies that enable facial recognition, fingerprint recognition, license plate reading, and such can be used for surveillance and tracking purposes. It's only a matter of a few keyboard strokes for someone observing at the right computer to know who—and where—you are.

It only stands to reason that advanced surveillance technologies will become the cornerstone of the Antichrist's grip on power. Using these technologies, and new ones being developed every day, he can identify and suppress any signs of dissent and eliminate opposition, leaving behind a landscape devoid of resistance. An intricate web of surveillance cameras and monitoring systems exists in essentially every corner of the world that can track the movements and activities of every individual. No one will be able to avoid the all-seeing eye of the regime, and any attempt to challenge its authority will be met with swift and severe consequences.

Through this extensive surveillance network, the Antichrist's regime will invade the private lives of citizens, mining every available shred of personal information: algorithms, analyzed behaviors, thoughts, and preferences. Any potential threats to the regime will be quickly identified and addressed. The privilege of individual privacy will be forfeited in exchange for the illusion of security.

4. Influencing Key Institutions

The Antichrist will manipulate and gain control over influential institutions, including governments, financial systems, media, and religious organizations. Through deception and cunning, he will ensnare world leaders, persuading them to yield to his agenda under the guise of progress and unity. Meanwhile, he will be facilitating his rise to power and establishing control over the world.

Financial systems will be pawns in the Antichrist's master plan. He will orchestrate a web of economic control, using vast wealth and intricate financial instruments to sway markets and destabilize economies at will. His influence will extend far beyond the boardrooms, penetrating the very heart of global finance. We can expect to see central bank digital currency (CBDC) replace physical currency, which is the first step in creating a currency that would monitor and control what you buy.

According to Bo Li, deputy managing director of the International Monetary Fund (IMF), this new money would be programmable. He says, "A CBDC can allow government agencies and private sector players to program, to create smart contracts, to allow targeted policy functions."[3]

This will be the first step in an evil plan to control everything people buy or sell.

5. FORCING COMPLIANCE

As the Antichrist's grip on the world tightens, he will set in motion a sinister plan to solidify his control over every aspect of human existence. He will impose on all individuals a global identifying mark, referred to in Scripture as the "mark of the beast." Those who refuse to receive this mark will be unable to buy or sell anything. Through skillful manipulation of governments and influential institutions, the Antichrist will lay the groundwork for the widespread adoption of this mark. It will become a symbol of allegiance to the regime and a requirement for participation in the global economy and daily life. Those who refuse to receive the mark will be cast out, isolated from the world they once knew:

> He causes all, both small and great, rich and poor, free and slave, to receive a mark on their right hand or on their foreheads, and that no one may buy or sell except one who has the mark or the name of the beast, or the number of his name. Here is wisdom. Let him who has understanding calculate the number of the beast, for it is the number of a man: His number is 666.
>
> —REVELATION 13:16–18

If this seems too farfetched, Keyo, a technology company, has launched the Wave+ vein scanner, a tool that uses biometric information to allow users to make payments with the wave of a hand. And JPMorgan Chase is testing a pilot program for a technology that would enable customers to make purchases with their face or palm prints. Doesn't that sound like what John the apostle wrote about in the Book of Revelation? That technology is already here.

6. PERFORMING SIGNS AND WONDERS

To add to the charisma, the cunning, and the deception the Antichrist uses to rise to world control, he will punctuate his presentations with miracles or supernatural feats to demonstrate his supposedly divine authority. Apparently, he will be a skilled con artist who will easily delude the crowds into following him. Scripture cautions us in many places to watch out for such tactics.

We looked at Jesus' warning earlier in this chapter, but it bears repeating in this context: "For false christs and false prophets will rise and show great signs and wonders to deceive, if possible, even the elect" (Matt. 24:24).

The apostle Paul alerts us to the coming of "the lawless one" (Antichrist): "The coming of the lawless one is according to the working of Satan, with all power, signs, and lying wonders, and with all unrighteous deception among those who perish, because they did not receive the love of the truth, that they might be saved" (2 Thess. 2:9–10).

So how does someone avoid being among those who will be taken in by this figure who wins people over with his charm and counterfeit spiritual credentials, who is so well polished that he deceives "even the elect"? The apostle John, who provides many specifics about this individual in the Book of Revelation, also wrote about him in his first letter to the churches. In 1 John 2, he warns of a preponderance of "antichrists" who will precede the coming of *the* Antichrist.

His advice is that the church today needs to be more alert to the spirit of antichrist wherever it arises and opposes the Spirit of God. At midnight, we need to remember that Christians are as sheep in the midst of wolves, and we need to heed Jesus' instructions to be "wise as serpents and harmless as doves" when interacting with a secular world (Matt. 10:16). We must clarify God's truth wherever we see it assaulted or misrepresented. As we get better at exposing the spirit of antichrist, whether spoken intentionally or in ignorance, we prepare ourselves and others to see more clearly and respond with greater boldness as each new day brings us closer to the last days.

Chapter 6

Threat of Demonic Infiltration

I F YOU ASK the average person on the street what they know about demons, you're likely to get a perception based on what they have seen on television or at the movies. Hollywood pumps out horror shows because, despite much lower budgets than action movies, they are more likely to make a profit. As one critic observed, "Fear is cheap....It's entirely possible to scare the hell out of an audience with little more than strange sounds, unexplained quick movements, and the mere suggestion of a terrifying monster or ghost."[1]

As such, demons—or at least the public's impression of demons—are big business. You can go online and find dozens of titles in the "best exorcism/demonic possession" category. As moviemakers attempt to make each film more shocking, more terrifying, and more profitable, viewers build up an immunity to being shocked or terrified by an elaborately conceived figure specially designed to invoke fear. They enjoy the show but may go home believing demons are no more real than any other movie bogeymen: vampires, werewolves, mummies, and such.

In our cultured, twenty-first-century American society, some people try to explain away the biblical accounts of demon possession. They suggest that what the uneducated people of first-century Judea were seeing was mental illness, which they didn't understand and therefore attributed to evil spirits. Yet on numerous occasions Jesus encountered those spirits, spoke to them, and cast them out of the person they had possessed.

C. S. Lewis presents an alternative perspective on demons in his classic satire, *The Screwtape Letters*. The book is a purported series of letters from an experienced demon (Screwtape) to a younger devil (Wormwood) who has been given the responsibility of leading his "patient" (a human being) to damnation. Using this tongue-in-cheek approach, Lewis provides many serious, thought-provoking observations about the real threat of the demonic world to humans—particularly Christians. In the preface of the book, Lewis observes: "There are two equal and opposite errors into which our race can fall about the devils. One is to disbelieve in their existence. The other is to believe, and to feel an excessive and unhealthy interest in them."[2]

The latter error (of excessive and unhealthy interest) is the Hollywood approach. But Lewis reveals a more insightful—and insidious—reason to be on the alert. Rather than recommending overt fear, the devilish Screwtape advises, "It is funny how mortals always picture us [demons] as putting things into their minds: in reality our best work is done by keeping things out."[3] In another letter, Screwtape suggests: "It does not matter how small the [human's] sins are provided that their cumulative effect is to edge the man away from the Light and out into the Nothing. Murder is no better than cards if cards can do the trick. Indeed the safest road to Hell is the gradual one—the gentle slope, soft underfoot, without sudden turnings, without milestones, without signposts."[4] In other words, the dark forces of evil rarely infiltrate their way into people's lives through terror and horror. They are much more covert, working slowly and methodically, which means they are even more a threat than most people realize.

DISCERNING DANGER

The Bible contains numerous references to demons, evil spirits, and supernatural entities seeking to gain power and control over humanity, leaving no doubt as to their reality. Yet Scripture is also abundant with passages reminding us that the power God provides is far stronger than anything the demonic world can muster against us. We must never forget that "He who is in you is greater than he who is in the world" (1 John 4:4).

One of the most well-known accounts of God's incomparable power is found in Jesus' encounter with a man possessed by a great number of demons. This story highlights the struggle between good and evil, emphasizing the power of divine intervention to cast out demons.

> Then they came to the other side of the sea, to the country of the Gadarenes. And when He had come out of the boat, immediately there met Him out of the tombs a man with an unclean spirit, who had his dwelling among the tombs; and no one could bind him, not even with chains, because he had often been bound with shackles and chains. And the chains had been pulled apart by him, and the shackles broken in pieces; neither could anyone tame him. And always, night and day, he was in the mountains and in the tombs, crying out and cutting himself with stones.
>
> When he saw Jesus from afar, he ran and worshiped Him. And he cried out with a loud voice and said, "What have I to do with You, Jesus, Son of the Most High God? I implore You by God that You do not torment me."

For He said to him, "Come out of the man, unclean spirit!" Then He asked him, "What is your name?"

And he answered, saying, "My name is Legion; for we are many." Also he begged Him earnestly that He would not send them out of the country.

Now a large herd of swine was feeding there near the mountains. So all the demons begged Him, saying, "Send us to the swine, that we may enter them." And at once Jesus gave them permission. Then the unclean spirits went out and entered the swine (there were about two thousand); and the herd ran violently down the steep place into the sea, and drowned in the sea.

So those who fed the swine fled, and they told it in the city and in the country. And they went out to see what it was that had happened. Then they came to Jesus, and saw the one who had been demon-possessed and had the legion, sitting and clothed and in his right mind. And they were afraid. And those who saw it told them how it happened to him who had been demon-possessed, and about the swine. Then they began to plead with Him to depart from their region.

—MARK 5:1–17

The scene is set in the region of the Gadarenes, where a man of tormented existence becomes the focal point of a spiritual battle. This man, possessed by many demons, finds himself dwelling among the tombs. The man's demon possession is marked by superhuman strength and erratic behavior, a manifestation of the malevolent forces that hold him captive. His cries and actions betray the inner turmoil that has consumed him, effectively imprisoning him within a life overshadowed by darkness.

This narrative not only portrays the man's suffering but also serves as a powerful depiction of the cosmic conflict between the forces of good and evil. The legion of demons that have taken hold of him represents the spiritual battles that rage unseen in the realms beyond the material world.

However, the heart of this narrative lies in the divine intervention of Jesus. When the man, tormented and crying out, sees Jesus from afar, he immediately approaches Him. As the man falls before Jesus, the demons within him recognize Christ and plead for mercy.

The exchange that follows underscores the sovereignty of Christ over the demonic realm. The man is not oppressed by a single demon but by a legion, an army of malevolent entities. (A Roman legion could vary from forty-two hundred to six thousand men.[5]) The request of the demons to be sent into a nearby herd of pigs further emphasizes their destructive nature.

Why did Jesus do as they asked? I believe it was because they were territorial spirits who were assigned to a region. One individual was freed from their oppression, yet the entire region needed to acknowledge the power and presence of God (Mark 5:19; Luke 8:39).

The subsequent events powerfully illustrate the ultimate authority of Jesus. Upon the demons' request, Jesus permits them to enter the herd of pigs, and the animals immediately rush into the sea and drown. As soon as the man is liberated from the grip of the demonic forces, the change in his demeanor is profound. He is found sitting, clothed, and in his right mind. This remarkable transformation serves as a visible testament to the power of divine intervention in breaking the chains of demonic captivity.

The reaction of the witnesses to this miraculous event is multifaceted. While some are awestruck and amazed at the restoration of the possessed man, others are overcome with fear and concern through the impact of Christ's power. The swine herders, who witnessed the demise of their pigs, respond with a mixture of astonishment and apprehension, leading them to share the extraordinary events with their community.

Jesus didn't merely heal the man physically; He liberated him from *spiritual* bondage as well. We must remember that we live under an open heaven, which means all the power and authority of Jesus are fully available to us. A short time after this event, Jesus gave His disciples "power over unclean spirits" and then sent them out in pairs to preach. They returned, reporting that they had cast out many demons (Mark 6:7, 13). Yet sometime later the group of them was unable to cast out a strong spirit who had control of a child, and Jesus had to heal the boy (Mark 9:17–29). This is a reminder of how dependent we are on God's strength. We cannot win the battle with human effort.

Territorial Warfare

Jesus, in His earthly ministry, walked in an unparalleled anointing, carrying the Spirit without measure. This divine empowerment defied the boundaries of human understanding. As believers, we are to act with spiritual authority over demonic forces that invade our communities, including our homes and schools.

The notion of regional demonization, though often debated, finds intriguing scriptural support that sheds light on the intricate dynamics of spiritual warfare. Within the pages of the Bible, glimpses of malevolent forces exerting influence over specific geographical areas emerge, painting a compelling picture of how those entities attach themselves to regions, nations, and even particular locations.

Daniel's Encounter: "The Prince of Persia"

The narrative in the Book of Daniel, for example, unveils a remarkable instance that hints at the existence of spiritual entities exerting control over regions. An angelic messenger sent to Daniel faces strong resistance from "the prince of the kingdom of Persia." This celestial clash reveals an unseen struggle between heavenly and demonic forces, where an evil spiritual prince appears to hold dominion over the Persian realm. This suggests an evil influence is woven into the fabric of that region, intertwining with its nation, people, and land (Dan. 10:12–13).

Diabolic Attachment to Geography: "Legion" and Pergamum

In the case of the man possessed by "Legion" (Mark 5:1–20), those demons pleaded with Jesus not to send them out of the region, implying an attachment to the geographical area they inhabited. This phenomenon hints at the complex relationship between malevolent entities and specific locations.

Further confirming this notion is the message in Revelation to the church in Pergamum. Jesus referred to this location as where "Satan's throne is" (Rev. 2:13). This intriguing phrase underscores the idea that certain regions can become focal points for demonic activity and influence, shaping the spiritual climate of the area.

Smyrna's Synagogue: A Place of Satan

Similarly, another church that received Jesus' message in the Book of Revelation was Smyrna. Jesus identified the synagogue in that city as "a synagogue of Satan" (Rev. 2:9), which illuminates the concept of diabolic attachment to specific religious sites. This assertion underscores the reality that spiritual forces can take hold even within religious institutions, signifying the extent of their influence.

PREVENTING DEMONIC INFILTRATION

When we become more attuned to the threat of malevolent spirits actively working to prevent or impair our relationship to a good and loving God, the next question is, "What steps do I take to counteract the potential for demonic infiltration?" Scripture offers much wise and helpful advice.

1. Spiritual discernment. To prevent demonic infiltration, it is crucial to cultivate spiritual discernment and maintain a robust prayer life. Discernment is a work of the Holy Spirit that enables believers to navigate with wisdom and insight in the spiritual realm. At its core, discernment is the art of distinguishing truth from deception, light from darkness. Through discernment we perceive the hidden currents of the supernatural, unveiling the intentions and movements of both light and darkness. By nurturing this discernment, we gain the capacity to recognize the subtle shifts, influences, and whispers that signify the presence of demonic forces seeking to infiltrate homes, schools, and churches.

2. Prayer. In addition to a commitment to nurturing spiritual discernment, we must maintain a robust prayer life. Jesus urged His followers to "Watch and pray, lest you enter into temptation" (Matt. 26:41). This admonition stands as a constant reminder of the need to remain vigilant in understanding spiritual dynamics and fortifying oneself against potential spiritual attacks.

3. Guarding the mind. The Bible places a profound emphasis on guarding the mind, recognizing its pivotal role in shaping our beliefs, emotions, and actions. The apostle Paul, in his letter to the Philippians, underscores the significance of this task: "Finally, brethren, whatever things are true, whatever things are noble, whatever things are just, whatever things are pure, whatever things are lovely, whatever things are of good report, if there is any virtue and if there is anything praiseworthy—meditate on these things" (Phil. 4:8).

Guarding the mind begins with the renewal of thoughts through the transformative power of Scripture. Romans 12:2 exhorts believers: "Do not be conformed to this world, but be transformed by the renewing of your mind." Regular engagement with God's Word enables us to dismantle negative thought patterns and replace them with truths that align with God's character.

4. Spiritual warfare. In the unseen realm where the forces of light and darkness engage in an eternal struggle, spiritual warfare emerges as the divine arsenal against demonic infiltration. Grounded in biblical principles, this concept acknowledges that the battle extends beyond the physical world and requires a comprehensive approach to thwart malevolent forces seeking to infiltrate and corrupt. Ephesians 6:12 encapsulates the essence of this warfare: "For we do not wrestle against flesh and blood, but against principalities, against powers, against the rulers of the darkness of this age, against spiritual hosts of wickedness in the heavenly places."

Following that verse, the next section of Ephesians provides a framework for spiritual warfare through the imagery of armor:

> Therefore take up the whole armor of God, that you may be able to withstand in the evil day, and having done all, to stand. Stand therefore, having girded your waist with truth, having put on the breastplate of righteousness, and having shod your feet with the preparation of the gospel of peace; above all, taking the shield of faith with which you will be able to quench all the fiery darts of the wicked one. And take the helmet of salvation, and the sword of the Spirit, which is the word of God; praying always with all prayer and supplication in the Spirit, being watchful to this end with all perseverance and supplication for all the saints.
>
> —EPHESIANS 6:13–18

This metaphor underscores the necessity of equipping oneself with divine defenses. The belt of truth serves as a foundational piece, guarding against deception and falsehood. The breastplate of righteousness protects the heart, while the gospel of peace readies one's feet to stand firm against the enemy's advances. The shield of faith extinguishes fiery darts of doubt, and the helmet of salvation guards the mind from infiltration. The sword of the Spirit, which is the Word of God, becomes the offensive weapon for battling against dark forces. In the war against demonic infiltration, believers stand on the assurance of ultimate victory. Revelation 12:11 proclaims, "They overcame him by the blood of the Lamb and by the word of their testimony." Through the redemptive work of Christ and the testimony of faith, believers emerge as conquerors in the ongoing spiritual battle.

5. Seeking community. Warfare is more than an individual endeavor. The spirits who comprised "Legion" and possessed the man in the story from Mark 5 had discovered that there is power in numbers, but the same is true for believers too. We need to remember that we're never alone in our struggle against the powers of this dark world. Spiritual warfare is indeed something that is expected of every individual believer, but we're in this fight together. As we respond individually to the commands of our Lord, we form a mighty, united force. Others are watching your back as you watch theirs. The early church knew this to be true: "Now the multitude of those who believed were of one heart and one soul; neither did anyone say that any of the things he possessed was his own, but they had all things in common. And with great power the apostles gave witness to the resurrection of the Lord Jesus" (Acts 4:32–33).

6. Meditating on biblical truths. Spiritual warfare is not to be taken casually. Jesus' disciples found themselves frustrated and confused—and probably embarrassed—when they couldn't overpower the demon who had control of the father's little boy (Mark 9:17–18). Jesus implied that some spiritual battles would be more challenging than others. He told them, "This kind can come out by nothing but prayer and fasting" (Mark 9:29). Sometimes it's not enough to have a working knowledge of Scripture. We need spiritual disciplines that connect us more securely to God. In addition to prayer and fasting, meditating on God's Word is a powerful strategy that should be implemented on a regular basis—not just when a distressing problem arises. Then anytime you need guidance from God, you'll have it hidden in your heart and you'll be better prepared to face any challenge.

Demonic infiltration, as portrayed in the Bible, underscores the spiritual struggle between good and evil. While the concept of demonic influence may seem daunting, the Bible also offers a wealth of guidance on how to prevent and address such occurrences. By cultivating spiritual discernment, maintaining a strong prayer life, guarding the mind, practicing spiritual warfare, seeking community, and meditating on biblical truths, individuals can effectively fortify their homes and schools against demonic infiltration. In doing so, they tap into the divine protection and guidance offered by their faith, strengthening their resilience against malevolent forces.

KEEPING THE HOUSE CLEAN

One of Jesus' teaching stories, sometimes referred to as the parable of the unclean spirit, carries a profound message about spiritual and moral cleanliness, as well as the importance of maintaining one's inner house to prevent potential relapses into darkness. This parable conveys a timeless lesson that holds relevance in both spiritual and practical aspects of life.

> "When an unclean spirit goes out of a man, he goes through dry places, seeking rest; and finding none, he says, 'I will return to my house from which I came.' And when he comes, he finds it swept and put in order. Then he goes and takes with him seven other spirits more wicked than himself, and they enter and dwell there; and the last state of that man is worse than the first."
>
> —LUKE 11:24–26

In this parable Jesus likens the human soul to a house. He speaks of an unclean spirit that leaves a person, seeking rest and finding none. This unclean spirit, unsatisfied in its search for a new host, eventually decides to return to its original dwelling. Upon returning, it finds the house swept clean and put in order. Initially, it may seem that the person had undergone a positive transformation—the house is tidy and free from the unclean spirit. However, the story takes a dark turn as the unclean spirit returns, bringing along seven more wicked spirits, and together they reenter and dwell within the house.

The initial cleansing represents a moment of transformation or personal growth—a period when an individual may overcome a specific challenge, addiction, or negative influence. However, the story emphasizes that merely removing the impurity or darkness is not enough. Without a commitment to filling that spiritual void with something wholesome, there is a risk of falling back into old patterns or attracting even greater negativity.

In practical terms, this parable can be applied to various aspects of life. It reminds us that breaking free from a harmful habit, toxic relationship, or destructive mindset is a significant step, but it is only the beginning. The process of personal growth and self-improvement requires ongoing effort and a conscious decision to replace negative influences with positive ones. It is not enough to remove the clutter from our lives; we must actively cultivate virtues, values, and habits that nurture our well-being and spiritual growth.

Moreover, this parable serves as a warning against complacency. The metaphor of the "swept and put in order" house underscores the danger of self-satisfaction after an initial triumph. Success in personal transformation should not lead to a sense of accomplishment that blinds us to the ongoing need for vigilance and self-improvement. Just as a clean house can attract more residents, a positive change can invite new challenges. Staying vigilant and committed to spiritual and moral growth is essential for lasting transformation.

In the context of spirituality and faith, this parable reminds us of the importance of an enduring relationship with God. It suggests that we should not only seek to remove the impurities from our hearts but also continually nurture our connection with the divine. We might be able to reduce or eliminate the amount of "dirt" we allow into our lives, but we must never become proud of ourselves and think, "Look what I did!" We can (and should) do our best to clean up our lives, but we should never forget that only God can fill that new clean space with His abundant goodness and grace.

The parable of the unclean spirit teaches us a valuable lesson about personal transformation, growth, and spiritual cleanliness. It emphasizes that cleansing our lives of negativity is just the first step. To prevent a return to darkness or the attraction of more significant challenges, we must actively cultivate positive qualities, remain vigilant, and nurture our spiritual connections. This timeless message encourages us to maintain our inner houses with care, ensuring they remain sanctuaries of light, love, and virtue.

In a previous book I included Jesus' words that preceded His warning about the unclean spirit who returns to the cleaned-out house:

> When a strong man, fully armed, guards his own palace, his goods are in peace. But when a stronger than he comes upon him and overcomes him, he takes from him all his armor in which he trusted, and divides his spoils.
>
> —LUKE 11:21–22

Satan is the strong man in this reference. He oversees an army of demonic forces, impedes the spiritual growth of believers, seeks to control world leaders, and seeks only his own power and will. Yet Jesus is the One "stronger than he" who will ultimately defeat him, judge him, and reclaim everything he thinks is his.

As we saw in this chapter, Jesus gives His followers authority over evil spirits (Luke 9:1; 10:17). As He did with His disciples, He still sends us out to represent Him in this world of chaos and evil. In His power we work to bind "the strong man" in every nation, state, city, neighborhood, school, and home.

Chapter 7

The Kings of the East: China in Biblical Prophecy

CHINA IN PROPHECY

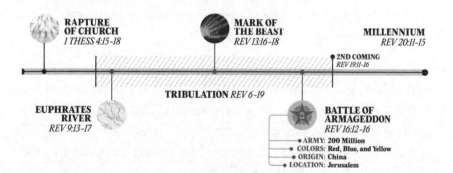

RAPTURE OF CHURCH
1 THESS 4:15-18

MARK OF THE BEAST
REV 13:16-18

MILLENNIUM
REV 20:11-15

2ND COMING
REV 19:11-16

TRIBULATION *REV 6-19*

EUPHRATES RIVER
REV 9:13-17

BATTLE OF ARMAGEDDON
REV 16:12-16

ARMY: 200 Million
COLORS: Red, Blue, and Yellow
ORIGIN: China
LOCATION: Jerusalem

A HEADLINE APPEARED IN the *New York Times* a few years ago that caught my attention, not because I follow climate patterns, but because I follow Scripture. It read: "Iraq Suffers as the Euphrates River Dwindles."

I was intrigued because I immediately thought of the biblical passage that predicted that very event. But what really stunned me was that the article's writer also knew about the prophecy:

The shrinking of the Euphrates, a river so crucial to the birth of civilization that the Book of Revelation prophesied its drying up as a sign of the end times, has decimated farms along its banks, has left fishermen impoverished and has depleted riverside towns as farmers flee to the cities looking for work.[1]

I was amazed to realize that one of the most well-known newspapers in the United States would make a connection between this natural event and the reference to its fulfillment tucked away among the end-times judgments described in Revelation. The writer knew what he was talking about. Here's the account from Revelation:

Then the sixth angel poured out his bowl on the great river Euphrates, and its water was dried up, so that the way of the kings from the east might be prepared.

—Revelation 16:12

The article went on to describe the effects of drought in Iraq but didn't pursue the biblical significance. The drying up of the great river was to allow easy access for "kings from the east" to move into the Middle East. It would be an enormous army, one that John had already described in his vision:

I heard a voice from the four horns of the golden altar which is before God, saying to the sixth angel who had the trumpet, "Release the four angels who are bound at the great river Euphrates." So the four angels, who had been prepared for the hour and day and month and year, were released to kill a third of mankind. Now the number of the army of the horsemen was two hundred million; I heard the number of them. And thus I saw the horses in the vision: those who sat on them had breastplates of fiery red, hyacinth blue, and sulfur yellow; and the heads of the horses were like the heads of lions; and out of their mouths came fire, smoke, and brimstone. By these three plagues a third of mankind was killed—by the fire and the smoke and the brimstone which came out of their mouths. For their power is in their mouth and in their tails; for their tails are like serpents, having heads; and with them they do harm.

—REVELATION 9:13–19

John was writing sometime around 90 AD when he foresaw this army of 200 million soldiers. At that time, it is estimated that the population of *the entire world* was around 100 million people. A force of 200 million soldiers would have been unfathomable when he wrote. To put that in today's context, in which there are roughly eight billion people on planet Earth, can you imagine someone predicting an army of sixteen billion people? They would seem like a fool, an eccentric, as crazed as Noah must have seemed building an ark before the world had seen a drop of rain.

The apostle John's number was astoundingly precise. As early as 1965, the nation of China reported a standing militia of 200 million.[2] Was this a coincidence? No, this demonstrates the accuracy of biblical prophecy. And John's detailed description contains other references to China. He describes seeing the colors of red, blue, and yellow. Red and yellow have been the colors associated with modern China since 1949. The military force of the People's Republic of China is the People's Liberation Army (PLA). Their military branches utilize the colors of red, yellow, and blue. The precise details of this prophecy are both accurate and alarming. John was writing about our day!

The terrifying imagery used to describe this army suggests that the soldiers are demon-possessed. To begin with, their supernatural attributes and the gruesome nature of their actions suggest a demonic origin. Additionally, the elements in the riders' breastplates—fire, hyacinth, and sulfur—are often associated with hell or the abode of evil spirits. And the presence of fire, smoke, and sulfur is often connected with divine judgment and punishment in biblical symbolism. Their presence here could represent the forces of destruction that the demonic army wields, possibly as instruments of God's judgment on the world. The characteristics of these soldiers (and their horses) go beyond the capabilities of ordinary human beings, and another possibility is that they will be genetically modified or even AI military bots.

THREATS FROM WITHOUT, THREATS FROM WITHIN

Researchers for the Jamestown Foundation say China is currently developing soldiers with "biologically enhanced" abilities, capable of running faster, jumping higher, hitting harder, thinking faster, and withstanding certain diseases, including genetically modified diseases that can attack enemy soldiers.[3]

According to Chinese general Zhang Shibo, former president of the National Defense University of the PLA, today's biotech advances make it possible to create new synthetic pathogens that are "more toxic, more contagious, and more resistant." A researcher from China's elite Academy of Military Medical Sciences says, "Obviously, genetic weapons possess many advantages over traditional biological weapons." But other researchers warn that "willful abuse of genetic weapons will bring unpredictable disasters to all mankind."[4]

Another, more pressing threat is China's collection of genomic and other health care data. We already know that since 2017, Chinese police have been collecting blood samples from men and boys across their country to create a vast DNA database of its approximately 700 million males for purposes of law enforcement and surveillance.[5] Now our own National Counterintelligence and Security Center of the FBI is telling us very plainly that the privacy of Americans is at risk.

When the COVID pandemic hit the United States, Washington state was the first to be affected. No sooner had the cases started to spike than Washington was approached with a proposal from BGI Group, the world's largest biotech firm, based in China. BGI offered to build and help operate state-of-the-art COVID testing labs while offering technical expertise, providing "high throughput sequencers," and making other donations. Bill Evanina, the top US counterintelligence official at the time, with backgrounds in both the FBI and CIA, issued a warning expressing alarm at the ability of foreign powers to collect, store, and exploit biometric information from COVID tests. In an interview a couple of years later, he warned, "Foreign powers can collect, store and exploit biometric information from COVID tests....This shows the nefarious mindset of the Communist Party of China, to take advantage of a worldwide crisis like COVID."[6]

Evanina's concern is that "the Chinese regime is taking all that information about us—what we eat, how we live, when we exercise and sleep—and then combining it with our DNA data. With information about heredity and environment, suddenly they know more about us than we know about ourselves and, bypassing doctors, China can target us with treatments and medicine we don't even know we need." Later in the interview he adds, "Current estimates are that eighty percent of American adults have had all of their personally identifiable information stolen by the Communist Party of China."[7]

The issue of genomic data collection by foreign powers, especially China, has become a pressing concern for national security experts and privacy advocates alike. The National Counterintelligence and Security Center (NCSC) of the FBI has warned about the risks associated with China's aggressive efforts to collect genetic and health care information of Americans. This collection is carried out through a variety of means, including cyberattacks, acquisitions of American biotech companies, and collaborations with US-based research institutions.

China's motive for collecting genomic data is multifaceted. The information can be leveraged for research in personalized medicine, biotechnology, and even for tailoring bioweapons. But beyond the immediate applications, the data gives China a strategic advantage. In an era where information is power, holding a comprehensive database of the genetic makeup of a large portion of the US population could offer an unparalleled advantage in various scenarios, from blackmail to influencing operations.

April Falcon Doss, who worked at the National Security Agency and wrote *Cyber Privacy: Who Has Your Data and Why You Should Care*, says that "Most Americans have probably had their data compromised by the cyber intelligence units of the Chinese government and Chinese military intelligence."[8] According to the *New York Times*, "China and other countries are trying to dominate these technologies, and are using both legal and illegal means to acquire American know how, said Michael Orlando, the acting director of the counterintelligence center, an arm of the Office of the Director of National Intelligence."[9]

Between Russian and Chinese hacking and their purchase of American biotech companies that exercise tremendous influence within our country, the privacy and security of Americans has never been more at risk. Moreover, the issue doesn't stop at hacking. China has also been buying stakes in American biotech companies. For instance, in 2018, China's iCarbonX, a digital life company, acquired PatientsLikeMe, a US-based health care startup. In 2019, however, the Committee on Foreign Investment in the United States (CFIUS) forced iCarbonX to divest its stake. Since then CFIUS and Team Telecom, which dispenses licenses for foreign telecommunications companies to operate, "have become more assertive—often retroactively ordering divestiture or revocation against Chinese companies, sometimes years after an investment was completed or a license granted. And notably, both committees seem to be broadly maintaining a similar posture under President Biden as under President Trump."[10] More concern is being shown for the extent to which China is willing to go to acquire health-related data.

The threat of biotech doesn't even begin to encapsulate the many ways China has encroached on the American way of life. It is common knowledge that China has been buying US farmland. Precise information is not always publicly disclosed or easily accessible, so an accurate figure for the total amount owned by China is difficult to determine. Additionally, the ownership of farmland in the United States can involve various legal and financial structures that may further complicate the process of tracking foreign ownership. But a reasonable estimate for US *residential* real estate is that Chinese buyers now account for 25 percent of the total foreign investment.[11]

The topic of foreign ownership of US farmland has long been a source of concern. Some foreign acquisitions have sparked debates about national security, food security, and potential impacts on local communities and the agricultural industry. According to the 2021 report from the Department of Agriculture, China owned 384,000 acres of US farmland. The fear is that if China can control our food production, they can control us.[12]

OF BONDAGE AND LIBERATION

In terms of sheer numbers and potential capabilities, the threat of China can sound intimidating if not downright horrifying, yet before we overreact also consider the amazing fact that amid this Communist atheistic regime, Christ has built His church.

It is estimated that the underground church in China numbers between 130 million to 150 million people.[13]

The term "underground church" refers to the unregistered or unofficial Christian gatherings that operate independently of the state-controlled religious institutions. God continues to bless and protect His church. Jesus reminded us that not even "the gates of hell" will prevail against it (Matt. 16:18, KJV). The church, comprised of all true believers, will ultimately prevail against all the forces of evil.

God will not abandon His people, and that includes the Chinese Christians. China has a prophetic promise found in the Book of Isaiah:

> That You may say to the prisoners, "Go forth,'" to those who are in darkness, "Show yourselves." ...He who has mercy on them will lead them, even by the springs of water He will guide them....Surely these shall come from afar...from the land of Sinim [China].
>
> —Isaiah 49:9–10, 12

Though the Chinese have lived in darkness and oppression since the country's commitment to Communism in 1949 under Mao Zedong, this bondage will be broken. Isaiah refers to them as prisoners who will "go forth" and be guided by the Lord. The Lord will show mercy on them and lead them by springs of water. We have seen that despite the challenges and risks, the underground church in China continues to grow and thrive during its persecution. It has become an emblem of resilience and faith in the true God of the Bible.

While we rightly celebrate freedoms in the West that we have achieved over time, the world is somehow strangely passive about the fact that our neighbors in the East are no closer to freedom than ever. No other ideology has so damaged, captured, and destroyed more people on planet Earth than Communism. Previous examples of Communist regimes include the Soviet Union under Joseph Stalin, China under Mao Zedong, Cambodia under the Khmer Rouge, and several Eastern European countries under Soviet influence. These regimes were responsible for large-scale atrocities and human rights violations, including mass killings, forced labor camps, and political purges.

Without minimizing the atrocity of six million Jews killed by Hitler, we reflect far less often on Mao Zedong and the *fifty million* Chinese that were killed. Weighing factors including genocides, extrajudicial executions, and artificial famines, Professor Mark Kramer at Harvard University suggests that "the total number [of people] who died unnatural deaths under communist regimes...[is] upward of 80 million."[14]

In China, the church is divided into two groups: the state-sponsored church (marching right in step with the Communist Party) and the underground church. Churches there really don't have freedom to preach the gospel, and they are specifically forbidden from preaching from the Book of Revelation. Why is that? Because the "kings of the east" rightly recognize that it is a powerful, dangerous thing for people to find their own lives and the lives of their rulers in the story of Scripture—when they do, they find freedom! The kings are shrewd enough, as are the demonic spirits behind the scenes, to know that the realities of Revelation would be disruptive to the order and control they have imposed.

Remember that the *whole* story of Scripture is relevant here, not just a handful of individual passages. Isaiah included prophecies about China in the same texts in which he also foretold the Messiah who would come. Similarly, the Psalms offer a prophetic glimpse into the future battle of Armageddon that will involve all the kings of the earth and their efforts to break the restraints of God:

Why do the nations rage, and the people plot a vain thing? The kings of the earth set themselves, and the rulers take counsel together, against the LORD and against His Anointed, saying, "Let us break Their bonds in pieces and cast away Their cords from us."

—PSALM 2:1–3

But why would they rage against the Messiah? The Messiah would be good, kind, loving, and just. Their rage and injustice will be unfair, as it was the first time when they crucified Jesus, rejecting the Son of love who had not only done nothing wrong, but had done everything He could to help, heal, and deliver. The reason all the kings of the earth rage is because they recognize the truth of what Jesus taught us—that you cannot serve two masters. They know that when their subjects bow to Jesus, it ultimately means they can't (or won't) bow to them. If Jesus is Lord, as the first-century Christians and their opponents knew all too well, then Caesar is not.

Earlier I mentioned that my wife and I were privileged to go to Romania in March 1990 to preach the Word of God and strengthen the churches, all of which had experienced years of persecution. Communist dictator Nicolae Ceausescu had been tried and executed on December 25, 1989, ending a long reign of terror, but the pall of Communism was still felt across the land. What we heard repeatedly from people was that Communism had destroyed the lifeblood of Romania. What had been the breadbasket of Europe prior to World War II was taken over by a despotic ruler, leaving devastation in his wake—as has happened everywhere in the world that Communism is followed.

The agenda of Communist China is world domination. China's agenda has been clear both in its actions and its goals. In addition to the insights provided in Scripture, extra-biblical sources warn of the aspirations of China. Nostradamus, a sixteenth-century mystic, prophesied that a great Asiatic empire would spread across the continents to destroy the Christian world. And Christian theologian Dr. John Walvoord wrote in 1967, regarding the coming power of the East, "The fact that the rise of Asia has occurred in our twentieth century with so many rapid and unexpected developments is another evidence that the world is moving toward its final climax and the end of the times....In Asia, as in other parts of the world, the stage is being set for the final drama in which the Kings of the East will have their important part."[15]

THE BOOK OF ELI

Among the many ways China restricts human freedom, not least among them is governmentally controlled access to the Bible. A few years ago, citing the rising costs of both printing and labor, American Bible publishers decided to outsource most of their publishing (about 85 percent of twenty million Protestant and Catholic Bibles printed annually) to China.[16] As it turns out, China's Amity Press now has a near monopoly on all the Bibles printed in the entire world, and Amity Press is under the wing of the Communist Party. China's intensified religious persecution of its people was already considered by US intelligence to be "the greatest threat to America today."[17] Several years ago they already "censored the Bible from the Chinese internet, banned youth from church services and Bible camps, and authorized the burning of Bibles possessed without state authorization."[18]

It gets worse. In 2018, Beijing announced the launch of a new plan to "retranslate or reinterpret" the Chinese Union Bible to make it conform to Chinese Communist Party policies—part of a five-year plan to "Sinicize" Christianity:

> Chinese Christian experts have reason to fear that the forthcoming version will drop the book of Revelations and distort moral lessons through new scriptural commentaries—the

account of Jesus forgiving the adulterous woman in John 8, for example, was already altered in 2020 Chinese textbooks (used in government-run secondary vocational schools) to claim that Jesus stoned the woman.[19]

As of 2020, Amity Printing was the world's largest Bible printing press, claiming to have printed over 200 million Bibles in more than 130 languages for over 140 countries[20]—all overseen by the Chinese Communist Party.

What would it be like if we no longer had access to the Bible? What if portions of it were deemed to be hate speech—or declared too subversive to our own state? What would that mean to us?

Spoiler alert: in the 2010 film *The Book of Eli*, set in a post-apocalyptic society, Denzel Washington plays a character who alone has a valuable book (a Bible) that others are trying to acquire for selfish purposes. They succeed in taking the Bible, but Eli connects with a group gathering holy books and other works of literature. They ask him, "Where is the book?," and he replies, "I am the book." Then he begins to recite it, word for word, line by line, to be transcribed. He had memorized the entire Word of God.

Scripture comes from an oral tradition and long predates our printing presses. As all the prophets of old knew, it was intended not to be read so much as memorized, rehearsed, meditated on, and hidden in our hearts.

Like twin rivers, the texts of Scripture and the texts of history flow toward their ultimate convergence, into the inevitable ocean that is the future. It was not John the Revelator but the feared general Napoleon who is credited with saying, "When [China] wakes, she will shake the world."[21] This has not always been the case. For years, China was perceived and described as a "paper tiger." But those days are long behind us, and we knew that the time of China's dominance was coming because Revelation foretold it. Even before there seemed to be any real threat, we knew the "kings of the east" would be coming.

And we know one other fact with certainty. Take another look at the passage from Revelation stated earlier in this chapter. We read that the "kings of the east" are coming some day in enormous numbers with a mandate to kill a third of humankind. Yes, they are coming someday, but not just any day. They are being prepared for a *specific* "hour and day and month and year" (Rev. 9:13–15). They are coming in God's timing, under God's control. Like every other threat we'll face in our lifetimes, we can be assured that God will provide all the courage, strength, and wisdom to withstand any obstacle and move forward in His power.

Chapter 8

The Days of Noah and the Days of Lot

WHEN JESUS SPOKE about the day of His eventual return, He made references to the days of Noah and the days of Lot, suggesting that the conditions and behaviors of the world in their time will reappear in the end times. These parallels serve as a prophetic warning about the state of humanity and the world before His second coming. Let's first look at what Jesus said, and then we'll delve into the events and characteristics of the days of Noah and Lot as described in the Scriptures to better understand the comparison.

> As it was in the days of Noah, so it will be also in the days of the Son of Man: They ate, they drank, they married wives, they were given in marriage, until the day that Noah entered the ark, and the flood came and destroyed them all. Likewise as it was also in the days of Lot: They ate, they drank, they bought, they sold, they planted, they built; but on the day that Lot went out of Sodom it rained fire and brimstone from heaven and destroyed them all. Even so will it be in the day when the Son of Man is revealed.
>
> —LUKE 17:26–30 (SEE ALSO MATTHEW 24:37–39)

The Days of Noah

Noah's era is described in Genesis 6:1–8. The world was steeped in corruption and wickedness. Not a lot of specific sins are listed in the text, but it seems safe to say that the world was much like the one the apostle Paul warns about in the last days when people will be "lovers of themselves, lovers of money, boasters, proud, blasphemers, disobedient to parents, unthankful, unholy, unloving, unforgiving, slanderers, without self-control, brutal, despisers of good, traitors, headstrong, haughty, lovers of pleasure rather than lovers of God" (2 Tim. 3:2–4). What we do know about the cumulative sin in Noah's day was that "the Lord saw that the wickedness of man was great in the earth, and that every intent of the thoughts of his heart was only evil continually. And the Lord was sorry that He had made man on the earth, and He was grieved in His heart" (Gen. 6:5–6).

"Lovers of themselves" appears to be a key phrase, denoting an attitude of extreme self-focus, hinting at a society that places personal desires and aspirations above the needs of others. This trait describes people who give in to their physical appetites and desires, are immersed in materialism, and disregard God and His commandments. This self-obsession exceeds mere self-care; instead, it dismisses or undervalues others while pursuing personal interests.

This trend has been magnified in our age of social media where platforms are often used to craft and project an idealized self-image. The relentless chase for "likes" and the proliferation of "selfies" illustrates the widespread shift in focus away from others' needs. As this attitude proliferated during Noah's time, humanity's wickedness and defiance were profound. God had warned that His tolerance for such sin would not endure indefinitely (Gen. 6:3).

Lawlessness had escalated due to increased demonic influence within society. Among the notable aspects of Noah's time were the Nephilim, often translated as "giants." These beings, born from the unnatural union of fallen angels and human women (Gen. 6:1–4), were a race of giants, indicating a profound distortion of God's creation. The rebellion of Lucifer and the fallen angels reached unprecedented levels of apostasy as they transgressed God's boundaries and pursued "strange flesh." Those fallen angels are now confined in hell, held in eternal chains under darkness until the final judgment.

As followers of Christ, we're called to be selfless and mission-oriented, to love our neighbors as ourselves (Matt. 22:39), and to esteem others above ourselves (Phil. 2:3). We are called to be vigilant, to live in righteousness, and to resist the pressures and influences of a world that increasingly resembles the days of Noah.

When Daniel interpreted Nebuchadnezzar's dream of a statue (a prophecy about a series of future kingdoms), the final kingdom was represented by the statue's "legs of iron, its feet partly of iron and partly of clay." Iron is often a symbol used in connection with the Antichrist, and here it is mixed with clay, representing human beings. This imagery could signify genetic engineering or transhumanism, hinting at a potential alteration of the "seed of men" in the last days (Dan. 2:31–44).

Transhumanism, a term introduced by Julian Huxley in 1957, suggests that humanity can and should surpass its current capabilities by "mixing with" advanced and emerging technologies. Elon Musk, a well-known advocate, argues that humans need to integrate with technology to avoid obsolescence amidst advanced machines. This stance, grounded in materialistic and often evolutionary perspectives, indicates a transhumanist belief that our present human form should be enhanced technologically or even entirely digitized, ultimately forsaking the physical body. Such manipulation could yield unanticipated consequences and further deviate from God's natural design.

Transhumanism's pursuit of human enhancement via technology presents intricate theological and ethical challenges. Among these concerns is the effect on the biblical concept of the *imago Dei* ("image of God") in humans. The doctrine of imago Dei affirms that humans are created in God's image, as Genesis 1:27 articulates. This principle is fundamental to Christian ethics, underscoring every individual's inherent dignity, worth, and value. The imago Dei forms the basis for human equality, the sanctity of life, and moral responsibility. Herein lie several concerns about transhumanism:

- *Alteration of God's creation.* If humans revamp their biology to a significant degree, they are tampering with God's creation. Some theologians argue that radical enhancements might alter or even erase the image of God within humans, violating the sanctity of life as divinely designed.

- *Humanity's unique role.* The image of God in humans is often associated with humanity's unique capacities, such as rationality, morality, spirituality, relationality, and creativity. If these abilities are artificially enhanced or replicated in artificial intelligence, it could blur the distinctiveness of humanity and challenge the unique role humans play as bearers of God's image.

- *Moral responsibility.* When cognitive enhancements or artificial intelligence are allowed to alter human decision-making processes, questions arise about moral responsibility. If humans are no longer entirely in control of their actions due to technological enhancements, how does that affect their understanding of sin, guilt, and redemption?

- *Equity and justice.* If only certain individuals can access enhancement technologies, it creates a significant disparity among humans. This inequity could be perceived as a violation of the biblical principle of justice and the equality inherent in the imago Dei.

- *False promises of salvation.* Transhumanism makes ambitious pledges about the potential for technology to offer a form of salvation. It posits that scientific and technological advancements can eventually overcome human limitations, including aging, physical and cognitive deficiencies, and even death. From a Christian perspective, these are false promises, redirecting hope away from God and toward human technological achievements—essentially a new form of idolatry. Human beings will never become the architects of their own salvation.

Viewed through a Christian lens, these grand promises of transhumanism are illusory, shifting our hope and trust from God to human achievements. Christian theology teaches that our ultimate salvation lies not in our own endeavors but in the redemptive work of Jesus Christ. It asserts that death has already been conquered through Christ's resurrection, and eternal life is offered to all who put their faith in Him. The assurance of salvation in Christianity is not about escaping or overriding our human limitations but about embracing our dependence on God's grace. It's about recognizing our human frailty and accepting the divine promise of eternal life. It's not about physically eliminating death but about understanding death in the light of Christ's victory over it.

While the church acknowledges the potential benefits of technology in alleviating suffering and improving quality of life, it must also beware the unregulated pursuit of transhumanism. Such caution encourages respect for the divinely bestowed dignity and value of each human being, promotes justice and equity, and upholds the unique role of humans as bearers of God's image. We are reminded that Christ suffered for our sins, providing the way for us to be reconciled with God. He will return one day, just as He promised, to gather His people and establish His righteous rule over all creation.

The days of Noah provide a prophetic warning for the end times. When we examine and compare them to our current times, the similarities are disquieting. Society today, much as in Noah's era, is predominantly guided by materialism, hedonism, and secularism. The rapid progression of technology has introduced unprecedented possibilities and brought with it a host of ethical dilemmas and moral quandaries.

These similarities between the days of Noah and the present day indicate that humanity is moving away from God's divine order and that judgment may be imminent. Disrespect for the institution of marriage, rejection of God's Word, widespread violence, corruption, pervasive illicit sexual behavior, blasphemy, and organized satanic activities are all reminiscent of the attitudes and behaviors prevalent in Noah's time. These parallels serve as a sobering reminder of the need for vigilance and commitment to uphold God's Word.

The significance of spiritual leadership in families and the church is of primary importance in these last days before the return of Christ. Wives are encouraged to submit to the husband's authority as a safeguard against the deceptions of the evil one

(1 Cor. 11:1–10). A caution is issued against an excessive fascination with angels (Col. 2:18-19), as this could open the way for a surge of demonic activity preceding the revelation of the Antichrist.

Considering these prophetic warnings, believers are called to remain steadfast in their faith, reject the allure of worldly pursuits, and seek a closer relationship with God. As the world grows increasingly chaotic, Christians must hold fast to the truth of God's Word and be a beacon of light and hope in the darkness. We are called to discern the signs of the times and live with spiritual vigilance. We should not be caught up in the pursuits of this world or be swayed by false teachings and ideologies. Instead, we must anchor ourselves in the unchanging truth of God's Word and remain steadfast in our faith. Like Noah, we are called to be faithful witnesses and heralds of God's truth in a world that often rejects it.

While the days of Noah carry a somber warning, they also convey a message of hope. The ark provided a way of escape and deliverance for Noah and his family, and in the same way God offers salvation and redemption through Jesus Christ. Those who turn to Him in repentance and faith will find safety from the coming judgment and the promise of eternal life.

The parallels between Noah's era and the present day call us to self-reflection and spiritual readiness. Just as God's judgment came upon the world in Noah's time, we can expect the return of Christ to bring both judgment and justice. So as we await His coming, let us live with purpose, seeking to honor God in all we do and sharing the good news of salvation with those around us. The days of Noah should remind us of the importance of living faithfully and obediently, holding on to the hope that Christ will return and set all things right.

The Days of Lot

Now we turn our attention to another account in the Book of Genesis. Lot was the nephew of the righteous man Abraham and lived in the city of Sodom. The Bible describes Sodom and Gomorrah as cities filled with great wickedness and immorality. The men of Sodom were exceedingly sinful before the Lord, committing acts of gross sexual immorality, violence, and perversion.

As we saw at the beginning of this chapter, "the days of Lot" are paired with "the days of Noah" in Luke 17—two prophetic warnings from Jesus, paralleled to make the same point about the end times. Understanding the significance of this comparison requires exploring the events and characteristics of Lot's days as described in the Scriptures.

Lot had left Mesopotamia with Abraham to settle in the land of Canaan, but when the land proved unable to support both men's large flocks and herds, they parted ways. Lot chose to live in the Jordan plain near the city of Sodom. One evening he was visited by two angels who had come to Sodom to investigate the extent of the city's wickedness. Recognizing the significance of these heavenly visitors, Lot welcomed them into his home and offered them hospitality and protection. However, the men of Sodom—"both old and young, all the people from every quarter"—surrounded Lot's house. Driven by their wicked desires, they demanded that Lot hand over the "men" so they could satisfy their immoral lusts.

In desperation, Lot offered his daughters to the mob instead, demonstrating the depth of moral corruption and depravity in Sodom. The angels intervened, striking the wicked men with blindness and urging Lot and his family to flee the city before it faced divine judgment. Despite the warnings, some of Lot's family hesitated, so the angels physically pulled out Lot, his wife, and his two daughters to escape the impending destruction.

As they fled, God rained fire and brimstone upon Sodom and Gomorrah, utterly destroying those cities and their inhabitants due to their unrepentant wickedness. These two cities that indulged in sexual immorality and pursued strange flesh were left in ashes as an example of the punishment of eternal fire for those who oppose God (Jude 1:6–7; 2 Pet. 2:4–6).

Now let us explore how the days of Lot relate to the present age and the end times:

- *Sexual immorality.* The prevalent sexual immorality and perversion in Sodom find parallels in the moral decay of contemporary society. Today's culture often promotes and celebrates sexual freedom without regard for God's design for sexuality within the bonds of marriage between a man and a woman. Homosexuality, adultery, and pornography have become increasingly normalized, echoing the sins of Lot's day.

  One example: in 1989, Marshall Kirk and Hunter Madsen, strategists from the gay community, released the controversial book *After the Ball* on public relations tactics for homosexuals to use in an active campaign to undermine the reasoning behind moral and religious standards. To them, this involved challenging conservative biblical interpretations hostile toward homosexuality. Furthermore, they encouraged the gay community to weaken the moral credibility of institutions that harbor homophobic beliefs, depicting any such institutions as outdated, regressive, and inconsistent with modern psychological understanding.

- *Violence and injustice.* Sodom was rife with violence and injustice. In many parts of the world today, violence and oppression are rampant, manifesting in wars, terrorism, human trafficking, and various forms of abuse. Innocent lives are often devalued or sacrificed, echoing the disregard for life evident in Lot's time.

- *Apathy toward God.* The people of Sodom had no regard for God and His moral laws. Similarly, many in the present age have grown indifferent or hostile toward God and His Word. We are seeing increasing rejection of absolute truth and a rise in secular humanism, leading people away from the divine moral framework. A recent Gallup poll confirms that a large majority of Americans still believe in God, yet the percentage continues to drop. Surveys taken in 1944, 1947, and twice each in the 1950s and 1960s recorded a consistent 98 percent of professed believers. By 2011, the number was down to 92 percent. In 2022 it hit an all-time low of 81 percent.[1]

- *Warnings and prophetic voices.* Just as Lot warned his family and the people of Sodom of the impending judgment, God continues to send prophetic voices and warnings through His Word and messengers today. However, many ignore or ridicule these warnings just as they did in the days of Lot.

- *Hesitancy and worldliness.* Even in the face of imminent destruction, Lot's family resisted leaving Sodom due to their attachment to worldly possessions and desires. Many people today are so entangled in pursuing material wealth and pleasure that they refuse to prioritize the eternal over the temporary.

- *Looming day of judgment.* The destruction of Sodom and Gomorrah is a powerful reminder of God's judgment upon unrepentant sin. The Bible also speaks of a future day of judgment when Christ will return to establish His kingdom and judge all humanity.

- *God's mercy and salvation.* Amid His judgment, God showed mercy to Lot and his family by allowing them to escape the destruction of Sodom. Similarly, God offers salvation through Jesus Christ to all who turn to Him in repentance and faith. Those who respond to His offer need not fear the coming judgment.

- *A remnant of righteousness.* No matter how much righteous people may be in the minority in a wicked and ungodly culture, we see from Lot's (and Noah's) example that God will protect them. He continues to have a faithful remnant of believers in the present age who strive to live righteous lives and uphold God's truth amidst a morally decaying world.

- *Final call to repentance.* The story of Lot stands as a final call to repentance and returning to God before the day of judgment. The Book of Revelation similarly calls for repentance and an invitation to receive God's grace before His final judgment falls upon the earth.

- *The role of the church.* Just as Lot was a witness for righteousness in Sodom, the church is called to be a light in the world today. The church's mission is to proclaim the gospel, call people to repentance, and demonstrate God's love and compassion in a world marred by sin.

The days of Lot serve as a profound warning and reminder of the consequences of unrepentant sin and rebellion against God. The similarities between the days of Lot and the present age highlight the urgency of our times and the need for spiritual discernment and readiness for Christ's return. In a world that echoes the days of Lot, the church has a crucial role in calling people to turn from sin, seek God's forgiveness, and find true life in Christ. The days of Lot serve as a solemn call to all humanity to heed the warnings of God and turn to Him before it is too late. Just as God rescued Lot and his family from destruction, He stands ready to offer salvation and eternal life to all who trust Jesus Christ. May we, as the church, be faithful in sharing this message of redemption and hope with a world desperately needing God's love and grace.

Christians are called to learn from the lessons of the past, discern the signs of the times, and live as faithful witnesses of God's truth and love. We must not be swayed by the moral decay and godlessness of the world but instead stand firm in our faith striving to lead lives of righteousness and holiness.

The story of Lot also reminds us of God's mercy and grace, offering salvation to all who turn to Him in repentance and faith. As the world continues to drift away from God's moral principles, it becomes increasingly crucial for believers to shine the light of Christ and share the message of hope found in the gospel.

Part III: A Look Around

Now that we've looked back to see where we've come from, and looked ahead to see what's in store in our future, it's time to take a good hard look at the here and now. On a national level, is America still the great nation our forefathers envisioned and designed? Is it still truly a land of liberty, or are some of the basic freedoms we've always known now being threatened?

On a personal level, how are you dealing with the changes you're beginning to see, even in America, that challenge rights we've always taken for granted? And if you are convinced that even more severe threats are on the horizon, what are you doing to prepare for them?

I suspect that too many people are shutting their eyes to anything they don't want to see, but problems are never resolved by doing nothing. Instead of looking away, take a closer look. As troublesome issues become more evident, only then will we be able to formulate a relevant and effective response.

Chapter 9

America Needs More Blacksmiths

A MERICA WILL CELEBRATE its 250th birthday in 2026. Or will it?

I'm beginning to wonder if we'll still be a nation by the time we celebrate that anniversary. Rabbi Daniel Lapin has been asking the same question. He has conducted a study of history and confirmed that when large numbers of people unite to build a society, their efforts seem to last an average of 250 years. Many of the dates can't be precise, but he cites several examples:

- Babylonian Empire (approx. 1780 BC to 1530 BC): 250 years

- Assyrian Empire (approx. 860 BC to 612 BC): 246 years

- Pax Romana of the Roman Empire (27 BC to 213 AD): 240 years

- Spanish Empire (approx. 1492 to 1742 AD): 250 years

- Pre-Communist Russian Empire (1682 to 1916): 234 years

- British Empire (1700 to 1950): 250 years

What's the significance of 250 years? Estimates for the length of a biblical generation can vary, but Rabbi Lapin notes with interest how in Genesis we see "ten generations" as repeated blocks of time: specifically, the ten generations from Adam to Noah (Gen. 5:1–29) and then from Noah to Abraham (Gen. 11:10–26). More than seeing generations merely as specific time spans, he observes the significance of the Hebrew names provided and discerns a pattern of how empires grow and then decline:

First Generation: bold breakout and conquest

Second Generation: commercial expansion

Third Generation: splendid buildings

Fourth Generation: widespread affluence

Fifth Generation: zenith and the best of days

Sixth Generation: extending influence beyond borders with money instead of military

Seventh Generation: rising political power of women and of the intellectual and academic elite

Eighth Generation: influx of foreigners

Ninth Generation: eat, drink, and be merry

Tenth Generation: internal political and civic fracture

He summarizes: "Each generation has a little less character strength than its preceding generation. Each generation's parents want their children to 'have it better than we did.' Invariably they mean materially, not spiritually. Additionally, each generation views the previous generation's luxuries as its necessities. Eventually, this seems to lead inevitably to a generation incapable of sustaining its own virility. The sad process typically takes about ten generations."[1]

But if you're talking about *democracies*, Rabbi Lapin's estimate of 250 years may be a little optimistic. Back around the turn of the nineteenth century, a Scottish lawyer and historian named Alexander Fraser Tytler was (most likely) the source of this observation:

> A democracy cannot exist as a permanent form of government. It can only exist until the voters discover that they can vote themselves largesse from the public treasury. From that moment on, the majority always votes for the candidates promising the most benefits from the public treasury with the result that a democracy always collapses over loose fiscal policy, always followed by a dictatorship. The average age of the world's greatest civilizations from the beginning of history has been 200 years. During those 200 years, these nations always progressed through the following sequence: from bondage to spiritual faith; from spiritual faith to great courage; from courage to liberty; from liberty to abundance; from abundance to selfishness; from selfishness to complacency; from complacency to apathy; from apathy to dependence; from dependence back into bondage.[2]

Do these patterns detected by Tytler and Rabbi Lapin sound familiar? If you look back into our history and review the courage and faith of our founders, and then return to our present governments and society, it doesn't take long to detect selfishness, complacency, and apathy, with underlying motivations of greed and lavish lifestyles. We appear to be at the tail end of a cycle that has eroded many empires of the past. Maybe we've come to expect that from our secular institutions. But I fear we're seeing this same pattern spreading through our churches.

Where Strength Is Forged

So as we approach our 250th year, is America already on borrowed time as a democracy? We might be, if we ignore the lessons of history and don't make any changes. I believe if the church leads the way in effecting change, it's not too late to reverse the decline, yet we need to face some hard truths.

I hear people saying, "I just want everything to get back to normal." By that, they usually mean easy, comfortable Christianity. I don't believe we'll ever go back to easy Christianity. Our faith must be more than a hobby in our lives, more than a tepid complacency where we expect God to bless us for what little commitment we show. It's time to rise up and be warriors for God—to prepare ourselves for battle.

I have a theory of my own: I believe America needs more blacksmiths.

The blacksmith used to be a respected and revered figure of society. Poet Henry Wadsworth Longfellow honored his local blacksmith with a poem, "The Village Blacksmith." It is a glowing tribute to the physical and spiritual strength of the neighborhood smithy. It opens with these lines:

> Under a spreading chestnut-tree the village smithy stands;
> The smith, a mighty man is he, with large and sinewy hands,
> And the muscles of his brawny arms are strong as iron bands. . . .
> Week in, week out, from morn till night, you can hear his bellows blow;
> You can hear him swing his heavy sledge, with measured beat and slow,

Like a sexton ringing the village bell, when the evening
sun is low.[3]

My granddad was a farmer who did his own blacksmithing to
make his tools. He took me out to the garage one day to show me
how to make a chisel. I never was very good at it, but I learned a
lot. We would heat up the coals to get them red hot while I put
on a mask and gloves. I would put the steel into the fire until it
was glowing and then pull it out and begin to pound it with a
hammer. When it started to cool, I'd put it back into the fire, let
it get red-hot again, and resume pounding. I quickly learned that
the blacksmith's job isn't an easy one, but it's still a necessary one.

The enemies of Israel realized the influence of a blacksmith
during the days of King Saul. The Philistines had invaded
and overrun Israel and implemented a strategy to prevent the
Israelites from rebounding:

> Now there was no blacksmith to be found throughout all
> the land of Israel, for the Philistines said, "Lest the Hebrews
> make swords or spears." But all the Israelites would go down
> to the Philistines to sharpen each man's plowshare, his mat-
> tock, his ax, and his sickle; and the charge for a sharpening
> was [two-thirds of a shekel] for the plowshares, the mattocks,
> the forks, and the axes, and to set the points of the goads. So
> it came about, on the day of battle, that there was neither
> sword nor spear found in the hand of any of the people who
> were with Saul and Jonathan.
>
> —1 SAMUEL 13:19–22

By eliminating all the Hebrew blacksmiths, the Philistines not
only ensured the Israelites couldn't produce new weapons, but
they also charged exorbitant fees for basic tool maintenance, which
imposed a financial burden. The absence of a blacksmith implies

a society bereft of its tools for change, defense, and progress. It's an image of vulnerability, subjugation, and loss of self-sufficiency.

The strategy of the enemy is much the same today. I see the godly pastors across our land as blacksmiths. They're the ones who are calling you to forge the swords, make the plows, and stand in the presence of God. If you remove the blacksmith, then there is no gathering place, no prophetic voice to be heard. An online voice in the air is not a sufficient replacement. A blacksmith with no fire has little to offer.

The blacksmith holds a symbolic significance that goes far beyond the literal. The profession itself is a craft that requires skill, strength, and meticulous attention to detail. As the blacksmith works, the raw material is transformed in the crucible of creation, under the hammer and against the anvil, in the heart of the forge.

The transformative processes of blacksmithing represent stages of character formation, resilience, and creative adaptation. Let's look at the basic elements.

1. **Forging** is the process of shaping metal through heat and hammering. In a metaphorical sense, life's trials and challenges are the heat that tests us, and our responses are the hammer strokes that shape us. We're formed and defined by how we respond to adversity just as the raw iron is shaped under the blacksmith's hammer.

2. **Bending** occurs when the metal is softened by heat, making it flexible and malleable. It symbolizes adaptability and resilience in the face of changing circumstances. In life, we often have to bend and adapt to new situations, changing our perspectives or strategies without losing our

fundamental essence, just as metal retains its nature despite its change in form.

3. **Welding** involves joining separate pieces of metal into a single cohesive whole. This stage can represent unification or the forging of alliances. Whether it's combining our strengths with others to achieve common goals or integrating various aspects of our personality into a harmonious whole, welding symbolizes unity and connection.

4. **Finishing** involves smoothing and polishing the forged metal, removing any rough edges or imperfections. Similarly, our personal development is an ongoing process of refinement, of continuously improving ourselves, smoothing out our flaws, and polishing our skills.

WEAPONS CHECK

Isaiah has more to say about the significance of the blacksmith. He portrays the blacksmith as a divine creation:

> "Behold, I have created the blacksmith who blows the coals in the fire, who brings forth an instrument for his work; and I have created the spoiler to destroy. No weapon formed against you shall prosper, and every tongue which rises against you in judgment you shall condemn. This is the heritage of the servants of the LORD, and their righteousness is from Me," says the LORD.
>
> —ISAIAH 54:16–17

In this passage, God says He is the one who creates the blacksmith, a figure who "brings forth an instrument for his work," symbolizing the human capacity for creativity, invention, and transformation. The blacksmith here is also a beacon of hope against "the spoiler to destroy," indicating resilience and the power to rebuild in the face of destruction. God may allow a potentially destructive "spoiler" to chasten His people when they go astray, but He always rules supreme. In His sovereignty, He assures us that no weapon forged against us will ultimately succeed.

The blacksmith metaphor thus captures the essence of personal and societal growth and transformation. It emphasizes our ability to shape our own destiny through resilience, adaptability, unity, and continuous self-improvement, regardless of the adversities we face. And in the larger context, it signifies a society's capacity for self-reliance, innovation, and sustained development.

The Philistines realized that by removing the blacksmiths from Israelite society, their subjects would remain helpless and unable to retaliate. A similar tactic is often employed by oppressive regimes that fear the power of an informed, united, and resilient populace. They understand that the most effective way to dominate is not solely through physical subjugation but through intellectual and spiritual subjugation as well. By removing the blacksmiths—metaphorically, the creative, transformative force—they leave a void, hindering societal progress and growth.

The enemy's strategy to remove the blacksmith as a means of conquering is a powerful metaphor for suppressing the tools and mechanisms of resistance in a society. This could take the form of censorship, limiting access to education, or stifling the voice of the people. By removing the blacksmith, the enemy attempts to ensure that the society cannot defend itself or form any substantive resistance.

The blacksmith in this metaphor embodies not only literal weapon-making but also the fostering of ideas, innovation, and resilience. He represents the capacity of a society or individual to adapt, change, stand firm in the face of adversities, and fight back when necessary.

BLACKSMITHS, FREE SPEECH, AND THE MODERN STRUGGLE FOR POWER

Historical anecdotes often have much to teach us about the dynamics of power and control. The Philistines understood that by removing Israel's capacity to forge weapons, they simultaneously stunted their ability to defend and possibly rebel against their oppressors. This strategy was not about the mere conquest of territory; it was about stifling the very tools and means of resistance.

Drawing a parallel to contemporary society, the realms of free speech, rights, cancel culture, and "fake news" present arenas of power dynamics that resemble that age-old tactic employed by the Philistines. In a world increasingly dominated by information and digital technology, the power to communicate, persuade, and influence is as potent as the swords and spears of antiquity.

Free Speech as Modern Weaponry

The role of free speech in modern democracies cannot be overstated. Like the swords, spears, and shields forged by blacksmiths of old, free speech acts as both a defensive and offensive tool. It defends citizens against tyranny, misinformation, and oppression, allowing for the free exchange of ideas, innovations, and progress. Conversely, it serves as a tool to challenge, critique, and protest established norms and authorities.

The Rise of Cancel Culture and Its Consequences

Much like the Philistines' strategic move to eliminate blacksmiths, the rise of cancel culture in modern discourse represents an attempt by some factions of society to curtail the weapon of free speech. Cancel culture, often manifesting as social ostracizing or professional repercussions for presenting controversial opinions, serves as a deterrent to free expression. While its proponents argue that it holds individuals accountable for harmful views, its unchecked proliferation can suppress genuine discourse, promote self-censorship, and create an environment of fear.

The Dual-Edged Sword of "Fake News"

Misinformation and fake news operate in this landscape as the counterfeit weaponry of the information age. Just as a poorly forged sword might break in battle, misleading or false information can shatter under scrutiny. However, its prevalence and speed of dissemination pose significant threats to informed discourse and democratic processes. The propagation of fake news can be likened to the Philistines not just removing blacksmiths but also leaving the Israelites with only inferior weaponry that would fail in critical moments.

Rights—the Anvil Upon Which Societies Are Forged

Fundamental rights, whether they pertain to free expression, assembly, or privacy, serve as the anvils upon which societies shape their futures. These rights, much like the indispensable tools of a blacksmith, enable citizens to mold, innovate, and reshape societal norms and values. Any attempt to curtail these rights, whether through overt legislation or covert surveillance, can be seen as a parallel to the Philistines' strategy—weakening the core foundational tools that a society relies upon for its defense and progress.

In drawing these parallels, it becomes clear that tools of power and control evolve, but the underlying strategies often remain consistent across ages. The Philistines, in their wisdom, recognized that to control a people, one must control their means of defense and resistance. Today, in the era of information, controlling narratives, speech, and rights serves a similar purpose.

The key to overcoming this strategy of the enemy lies in recognizing the value of our blacksmiths and safeguarding them. It's about nurturing the elements of society that foster critical thinking, innovation, and resilience. This could mean emphasizing education, supporting freedom of speech, promoting scientific and technological research, or fostering a culture of open dialogue and mutual respect. When we protect our blacksmiths, we secure our capacity for self-defense, resistance, and ultimately our freedom.

It is vital, now more than ever, to recognize these dynamics and ensure that the tools of free speech, the right to information, and other fundamental rights remain robust and accessible. Like the Israelites, who must have yearned for the return of their blacksmiths, modern societies must cherish, protect, and defend the tools and rights upon which their freedom and future depend.

History has shown that the spirit of the blacksmith—the spirit of resilience, creativity, and protection—often proves indomitable. The removal of one blacksmith might spark the rise of many more, fanning the embers of resistance into a blazing fire. The strength of a society lies in its ability to keep the metaphorical forge burning, to continue to shape and reshape itself in the face of adversity, and to turn the very weapons of the enemy into tools for liberation.

THE POWER OF TRUTH

So we're back to our question: Is America on borrowed time? Are we destined to follow Rabbi Lapin's and Alexander Tytler's predictions? Or will enough "blacksmiths" become vocal enough to make a difference in our increasingly secular society?

Prior patterns of civilizations, societies, and individuals serve as a poignant reminder of the impermanence of empires and the cyclical nature of human history. Yet they also underscore the unyielding power of the individual and the collective, armed with faith, courage, and truth to resist, reform, and rebuild in the face of adversity. From the ashes of decline, new civilizations arise, new societies are formed, and the cycle continues. The blacksmith's forge is never extinguished; it is merely passed on to the next generation, the flame of resilience flickering eternally.

A quote (frequently attributed to George Orwell, but unproven) encapsulates the climate of our current society perfectly: "In a time of universal deceit, telling the truth is a revolutionary act." Truth becomes the ultimate weapon, a beacon in the fog of deception and dishonesty, yet truth tellers are often met with opposition, painted as revolutionaries or troublemakers.

In response, some would say that troublemaking may be necessary at times to effect change. John Lewis was a civil rights activist who marched with Martin Luther King. He was among the "Big Six" leaders who suffered personally for their commitment to end racial segregation. Among other protestors, he was attacked and beaten on Bloody Sunday when they attempted to cross the Edmund Pettus Bridge on a march from Selma to Montgomery, Alabama. He is remembered for his sacrifice, his seventeen terms in the House of Representatives, and his philosophy: "Do not get lost in a sea of despair. Be hopeful, be optimistic. Our struggle is not the struggle of a day, a week, a month, or a year, it is the struggle of a lifetime. Never, ever be afraid to make some noise and get in good trouble, necessary trouble."[4]

"Good trouble" refers to civil disobedience in pursuit of moral justice and necessary reform. Lewis' words created a legacy of courage and resilience, encouraging others to challenge norms, question authority, and strive for justice even when it's uncomfortable, even when it means making some noise and inviting trouble. The kind of trouble that agitates the stagnant waters of complacency, prompting action and fostering change, is both "good" and "necessary."

Lewis underscores the importance of standing up for what you believe. He challenges us to not be afraid of causing a stir or disruption when it comes to fighting for justice, equality, and the truth.

If we want our nation to continue to its 250th year and beyond, we need more blacksmiths to emerge in our tumultuous landscape—not just as a maker of weapons, but as a symbol of steadfastness, creation, and renewal. Forging, bending, welding, finishing—these actions define the process of building resistance, of creating change, yet there is always the threat of the blacksmith's absence, a warning of a society left defenseless, without tools or weapons for survival, much less revival.

Longfellow's poem closes with some lines that may inspire us to remember the pastors, educators, and other "blacksmiths" in our lives who help us forge the tools and weapons to succeed despite the many challenges and setbacks of life:

> Toiling,—rejoicing,—sorrowing, onward through life he
> goes;
> Each morning sees some task begin, each evening sees it
> close;
> Something attempted, something done, has earned a night's
> repose.
> Thanks, thanks to thee, my worthy friend, for the lesson
> thou hast taught!
> Thus at the flaming forge of life our fortunes must be
> wrought;
> Thus on its sounding anvil shaped each burning deed and
> thought.[5]

Chapter 10

America Is in Biblical Prophecy: The Three City-States

ONE-WORLD GOVERNMENT

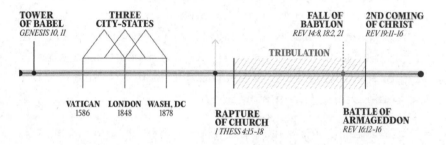

THE WORLD IS not falling apart; the world is falling into place. We are living in the best days of recorded history.

You may wonder how I can make such a statement. I can hear your protests: "Look around. Don't you see the injustice throughout the world, the decline of common courtesy and social graces, the lack of respect for one person toward another, the greed, the corruption, the sheer evil of human trafficking, drug addiction, gang rule, and more? This world, to borrow a phrase from a children's book, is a 'terrible, horrible, no good, very bad' place!"

The prophet Habakkuk found himself in a very similar situation. He opens his book with this complaint:

> O Lord, how long shall I cry, and You will not hear? Even cry out to You, "Violence!" and You will not save. Why do You show me iniquity, and cause me to see trouble? For plundering and violence are before me; there is strife, and contention arises. Therefore the law is powerless, and justice never goes forth. For the wicked surround the righteous; therefore perverse judgment proceeds.
>
> —Habakkuk 1:2–4

So if you find it difficult to make any sense out of what is happening in our world, know that you are not alone. But like Habakkuk, the best option you have when you're up to your chin in frustration and fear is to turn to God. The Lord sees what His people are going through and always has a plan to do what is best for them. When Habakkuk laid out his perspective to God, the Lord revealed His in return:

> Look among the nations and watch—be utterly astounded! For I will work a work in your days which you would not believe, though it were told you.
>
> —Habakkuk 1:5

When I suggest that we may be living during the best period of human history, it is based on the fact that we are living in the fullness of the Spirit, the fullness of revelation (the Bible is complete), and the fullness of the times. Never has a generation experienced such power, understanding, and fulfilled prophecy.

God is not absent. He is working "all things…together for good to those who love God, to those who are the called according to

His purpose" (Rom. 8:28). God has a plan that far exceeds our ability to understand, but He has given us the Word of God and the Spirit of God, so we are not left in the dark.

Biblical prophecy is a bit like a jigsaw puzzle; you must locate the pieces and then fit them appropriately to see the big picture of what God is doing. Most people think biblical prophecy is primarily clustered in the Books of Revelation and Daniel, but if you look no further than that, your puzzle will be too full of holes to make much sense. Prophecy is found throughout the entire Word of God. Prophecy is more than the outer edges of the story. It is the whole story and must be taken as a whole.

As important as the haunting dreams of Daniel and the dazzling visions of John the Revelator might be, those are not our starting points. As with all great stories, it is essential to pay attention as soon as the story of Scripture begins, so let's revisit the beginning.

ZOOMING OUT

Let's suppose our story of biblical prophecy were presented as a film (and the apocalyptic, panoramic imagery of Revelation in particular does unfold in a way that feels cinematic). To get the viewers' attention, many films open with scenes that don't make sense at first. We are cast into an unfamiliar setting even before the opening credits. So this film of biblical prophecy might begin with a widescreen shot of Vatican City with a fade into a shot of London, followed by another fade into Washington, DC. Now we're curious and wonder how the disparate images are somehow connected.

One city-state we associate with pontiffs, cardinals, holy men, and travelers who have come on pilgrimage for a blessing. We may imagine the sights and smells of liturgical worship—incense, prayers chanted in Latin, or the drama of midnight mass leading into Easter. The second city-state reminds us of international commerce and fashion, depicted in shades of gray due to its frequent rain, austerity, and old-world elegance. The third city-state is associated with its rebellion against the previous city-state and offers a great contrast to it, with its colonial architecture, unending traffic, and fast-talking politicians with much less posh-sounding accents.

Tertullian, a Christian writer who lived at the turn of the third century, famously asked, "What hath Athens to do with Jerusalem?" We could rightly ask the same about Vatican City, London, and Washington, DC. These three cities are as cosmetically, aesthetically, and culturally different as you can imagine. Geography and culture aside, what they do hold in common is influence over global politics and commerce—but the plot to our movie hasn't reached that point yet.

Instead of forcing some coherence to these diverse images too quickly, we follow the camera as it pulls back and suddenly zooms across both history and time, arriving back at that Hebrew book of beginnings we know as Genesis. We don't yet see diverse centers of power, control, and influence—not even any semblance of civilization as such.

The human project that unfolded after Adam and Eve's expulsion from Eden continued to get worse and worse. Cain killed his brother Abel (Genesis 4), and rampant defiance of God continued to spread until "the LORD was sorry that He had made man on the earth, and He was grieved in His heart" (Gen. 6:6). Judgment came with the great flood, and God gave humanity a fresh start, instructing them to "be fruitful and multiply, and fill the earth" (Gen. 9:1), yet almost immediately people returned to systemic sin and defiance against God.

Rather than "filling the earth" and establishing civilizations throughout, our camera reveals only one kingdom, only one language, only one speech. This first human kingdom includes Babel (or Babylon) on the plain of Shinar (Gen. 10:10). Its founder was Nimrod, whom Scripture refers to as a "mighty one on the earth" (10:8).

Defying God's clear (and repeated) instructions to spread out, the people decide to cluster and pursue their own grandiose dreams. The camera holds on a large work crew at the base of a structure and slowly tilts up to reveal a large tower under construction as a voiceover explains:

> Now the whole earth had one language and one speech. And it came to pass, as they journeyed from the east, that they found a plain in the land of Shinar, and they dwelt there.... And they said, "Come, let us build ourselves a city, and a tower whose top is in the heavens; let us make a name for ourselves, lest we be scattered abroad over the face of the whole earth." But the LORD came down to see the city and the tower which the sons of men had built. And the LORD said, "Indeed the people are one and they all have one language, and this is what they begin to do; now nothing that they propose to do will be withheld from them."
>
> —GENESIS 11:1–6

Being created in the image of their Creator God, the human drive to make things that dazzle and impress is there right from the start. Power and subjugation are the ends of humanity—even in the beginning. But therein lies the problem: people aren't God. When they seek God's power and protection, He amply provides it. But without it, no amount of collective human strength and determination will succeed.

God always gives people the capacity to choose, so for a time at least, God allowed them to have what they wanted. The civilization at Babel continued their project of building, consolidating, striving, and dominating. This is the default setting for what the human quest for power looks like, and this is where the story will always return—in biblical times and in our own. But when God determined, all He needed to do was confuse their language to induce them to scatter—reluctantly, against their will. We see that God's will ultimately is accomplished against all opposition.

The trajectory of the story is set—Babylon, in origin, is the model of a one-world government, the quest to consolidate human power under a single global leader. While it is not until many centuries later that we have reference to an "antichrist," this was always where the story was going. A unified world government—what we sometimes now refer to as a new world order—was the arc of the story Scripture was telling us from the beginning.

The camera shifts again, returning us from our journey through time and space back into the world as we know it, specifically to the three city-states from which we started. Still viewing those locations through a long lens, we don't at first detect any reflection of ancient Babylon. After all, doesn't the importance of city-states such as Vatican City, the City of London, and Washington, DC, seem almost negligible in the grand scheme of global politics? Can't you think of numerous other cities more noted for dominance and prestige? Yet these three hold unique positions of power and influence that contribute to the broader narrative of global governance.

As with watching any great film, we need to be attentive to *the details* to detect the cosmic drama unfolding in front of us. As the camera zooms closer and closer, these three cities are not quite as divergent as they may have first appeared. They have common bonds that will surprise us. The screen divides into three parts as we see, side by side, that each of the three city-states has its own flag, police force, and government. Each is a separate entity unto itself. And each one features an obelisk as a dominant architectural feature, representing the Egyptian sun god, Ra.

The scene flickers, and we glimpse something of the world as John saw it, where the narratives of the past, present, and future all converge. The separateness of these cities is illusory—the discrete images begin to come together as one.

VATICAN CITY—RELIGIOUS CENTER

Informed by the sacred history of Scripture, we zoom in first to present-day Vatican City, renowned as the spiritual and administrative headquarters of the Roman Catholic Church. With its own distinct government, flag, and military force—the Swiss Guard—Vatican City operates independently from Italy and other nations. It possesses significant wealth and extensive property holdings, including gold reserves stored in the Bank of England and the United States Federal Reserve Bank.

The obelisk in Vatican City is known as the Obelisk of St. Peter's Square. It stands prominently in the center of the square, serving as a focal point and a visual representation of the grandeur and spiritual significance associated with the Vatican. Its history can be traced back to ancient Egypt. Originally erected in Heliopolis during the reign of Pharaoh Seti I around 1290 BC,[1] the Obelisk of St. Peter's Square now serves as a symbolic landmark within the city-state.

In 37 AD, the Roman emperor Caligula ordered the obelisk to be transported from Egypt to Rome. In 1586, Pope Sixtus V had the obelisk moved to its current location in St. Peter's Square.[2] It seems strange that an Egyptian obelisk dedicated to the sun god would be placed in Vatican City, especially given the words of the prophet Jeremiah, "He shall also break the sacred pillars... that are in the land of Egypt; and the houses of the gods of the Egyptians he shall burn with fire" (Jer. 43:13).

City of London, Incorporated— Economic Center

Next we pan to the second city-state, the City of London, Inc., and we immediately sense we are encountering a very different place. While Vatican City is primarily associated with religious influence, the City of London is synonymous with financial power. Spanning just one square mile, it is the historic center of London and houses prominent financial institutions such as the Bank of England, Lloyd's of London, and the London Stock Exchange. Considered a global financial hub, the City of London wields substantial control over financial and monetary systems throughout the world. Its influence extends beyond the borders of the United Kingdom, shaping economic policies and practices worldwide.

In terms of governance, the City of London has a distinct system that differs from the rest of the United Kingdom. It is governed by the Lord Mayor, who is elected annually and represents the interests of residents and businesses within "the City." The historical origins of the City of London Corporation date back to medieval times. Over the centuries, the city has preserved its autonomy and continues to operate under its own rules and regulations, distinct from those of the wider country. This arrangement allows the City of London to maintain its identity as a financial and commercial powerhouse, with the flexibility to adapt and respond to the ever-changing demands of the global economy.

The City of London Corporation, the local governing body, operates independently of England with its own rules and government, including the Court of Common Council and various committees responsible for overseeing different aspects of city administration. The city has its own police force and maintains its own jurisdiction within its boundaries.

The City of London is known for its rich history and symbolic landmarks. Among the most notable is Cleopatra's Needle, one of a pair of obelisks that were originally erected in ancient Egypt during the reign of Pharaoh Thutmose III around 1450 BC. The transportation and installation of the obelisk in London's Victoria Embankment Gardens took place in 1878.[3]

Obelisks have long been associated with power, symbolism, and monumentality in various cultures throughout history. In ancient Egypt, obelisks represented the rays of the sun and were believed to symbolize divine power. Cleopatra's Needle carries with it the weight of history and a connection to an ancient world of grandeur and mystique. Its presence in the heart of the City of London holds both historical and symbolic significance. The inclusion of the obelisk can be perceived as a testament to the city's long-standing cultural connections with ancient civilizations. It serves as a reminder of London's longstanding and ongoing importance as a hub of financial power and economic dominance.

WASHINGTON, DC—MILITARY CENTER

Finally, the camera zeroes in on the third city-state: Washington, DC, the capital of the United States. This city-state operates autonomously from the rest of the country. The Constitution allows for a federal district under the exclusive jurisdiction of Congress. As such, Washington, DC, is neither a state nor part of any US state.

With its own flag featuring three stars—which I believe represent the three city-states—Washington, DC, holds immense political and military power. Its role as a superpower is undisputed and will play a significant role in the Babylonian system of the last days.

Americans often think of themselves as an ahistorical people, as if we didn't come from any particular people or places, disconnected from all that has come before us. But as we have followed our camera shots back and forth from ancient Babylon, to the civilizations that came in its wake, to Western civilization now, we are confronted with images that beg significant questions. The Washington Monument, another Egyptian-style obelisk, is the tallest obelisk in the world (at 555 feet) as well as the tallest structure in Washington, DC. The monument's cornerstone, a twelve-ton slab of marble, was donated by the Grand Lodge of Freemasons. Once again, we have to ask: Why does our nation's capital feature a monument to the sun god Ra?

The existence of these three city-states raises intriguing questions about their collective impact on global governance. Some theorists speculate that they represent centers of power within a larger network of control, with each city-state contributing to the overarching agenda of a new world order. The presence of obelisks in Vatican City, the City of London, and Washington, DC, further fuels conjecture because these ancient structures are historically associated with power across different cultures.

A PLOT TWIST

So far we've seen that from the time of Nimrod (Genesis 10) our world system has opposed God. It sought to corrupt God's people from the beginning and continues to oppose the true church. So at this point the camera moves from the past and the present to flash forward into the future. Although city-states such as Vatican City, the City of London, and Washington, DC, highlight the existence of distinct power centers for a one-world government, we see clearly that they will collapse, along with the entire Babylonian system. The Book of Revelation refers to the division and judgment of this evil system that stands in opposition to God:

> Now the great city was divided into three parts, and the cities of the nations fell. And great Babylon was remembered before God, to give her the cup of the wine of the fierceness of His wrath.
>
> —REVELATION 16:19

In this prophetic glimpse of the world to come, Babylon in all its historical incarnations is judged. All its power, riches, and influence are destroyed forever. The control of Vatican City, the City of London, and Washington, DC, are no more. The spell is now broken, and God's judgment—described as "the fierceness of His wrath"—begins to unfold.

Because the world has operated under the control of these same powers for so long, we can scarcely imagine a future in which they no longer rule and dominate. Revelation chapters 17 and 18 provide more details. The scope of Babylon's influence is seen in its name: "Babylon the Great, the Mother of Harlots and of the Abominations of the Earth" (Rev. 17:5). The influence of Babylon has in fact been vast, pervasive, seemingly almost comprehensive—but not infinite. In the same way that the tower project of Genesis was destined to fail, Babylon's persistent hubris, pride, and arrogance will ultimately lead to its final upending. We flash forward again to a climactic scene in the future:

> Babylon the great is fallen, is fallen, and has become a dwelling place of demons, a prison for every foul spirit, and a cage for every unclean and hated bird! For all the nations have drunk of the wine of the wrath of her fornication, the kings of the earth have committed fornication with her, and the merchants of the earth have become rich through the abundance of her luxury.
>
> —REVELATION 18:2–3

It's no spoiler alert to tell you that at the moment the merchants of the earth are not doing poorly. Babylon is big business, and those that indulge in her vices, drinking "her wine," enjoy power and pleasure for a season. The power of Babylon to rule over human systems may currently appear endless to us. The stock on Babylon has only ever risen. The same systems that prevailed and dominated from the beginning have only continued to ascend to a point where most people can't even imagine a descent. Merchants have learned that it's never a good idea to bet against "the house" upon which all our global systems are built.

Yet as certain as it is that Babylon's story had an origin, a place from which it all started, it also has a finale. We discover this in a shocking, unexpected plot twist:

> Then a mighty angel took up a stone like a great millstone and threw it into the sea, saying, "Thus with violence the great city Babylon shall be thrown down, and shall not be found anymore."
>
> —Revelation 18:21

Just before the final credits roll on this movie that's playing out before our eyes, Revelation shows us an image of a future in which Babylon not only *falls* down—it is *thrown* down. The kings and merchants that had for centuries profited from callous and corrupt world systems are left mourning in grief and despair. Despite its long history of power and prestige, Babylon is destroyed "in one hour" (Rev. 18:19).

Empires do fall, as hard as it is for us to imagine while we are living through them. We often see just some of the facts of history, leading us to believe that "you can't beat the system." The incredible influence and success of "Babylon"—both past and present—seem assured and undefeatable. But through the widescreen panorama of Scripture, starting from Genesis and moving all the way to the final judgment in Revelation, we see the inevitable end of any individual, any city-state, any nation, any empire, or any world system that stands opposed to God and His people. We have been shown the whole story, past and future, and it should affect how we live here and now.

Chapter 11

Persecution in America

ACH YEAR THE organization Open Doors ranks the 50 countries where Christians face the most extreme persecution. In the recently released 2023 World Watch List, those 50 countries are responsible for 312 million of the total 360 million Christians worldwide who are severely persecuted and discriminated against for their faith. Included in those numbers are 5,621 murders of Christians, 2,110 churches attacked, and 4,542 Christians detained.[1]

What that means is that one in seven Christians worldwide are persecuted. Within Africa, the numbers are one in five; in Asia, two in five. Ironically, the annual Christian population growth rates since 2000 have been highest in Africa (2.76 percent), followed by Asia (1.62 percent). At the bottom of the list are the United States (0.29%) and Europe (0.04%).[2]

Why is it that in the parts of the world where people are being brutally persecuted and killed, Christianity is thriving—whereas in America, a nation built on Christian values and character, growth has essentially stopped? You might also ask yourself, "Could Christians in America ever face such persecution?" Some people who've been watching the news closely over the past couple of decades suggest the first stages of persecution have already begun.

THREE EXAMPLES

As a diverse and multicultural society, the United States has historically prided itself on promoting religious freedom and tolerance. Christianity, the predominant religion in the country, has enjoyed widespread acceptance and played a significant role in shaping American culture and values. However, various factors and shifting societal dynamics have sparked concerns about the potential for the persecution of Christians in America.

Jack Phillips

You may have heard of Jack Phillips, a Colorado baker who owns and has operated a cake shop since 1993. After his decision to become a Christian, he called his business Masterpiece Cakeshop because "the very name of Jack's shop...not only reflects that Jack designs artistic cakes but also is a constant reminder that he operates his business in service to his ultimate Master—Jesus Christ."[3]

Phillips determined not to bake cakes that conflict with his strong religious beliefs. He and his shop received national attention in 2012 when he declined to create a wedding cake for a couple celebrating a same-sex marriage. The case went all the way to the Supreme Court in 2018, where the court decided in Phillips' favor in a 7-2 ruling.

But in 2017, on the same day the Supreme Court had agreed to hear his case, Phillips found himself in a new legal conflict. An attorney, Autumn Scardina, called and spoke to Phillip's wife, who agreed to sell her a pink cake with blue icing. Only later did the attorney reveal that the cake was to celebrate her gender transition from male to female. When Phillips refused to endorse the message of the cake, the lawyer sued, and the case has been in the courts ever since—most recently in January 2023 when a Colorado Court of Appeals panel ruled against Phillips' appeal in the case.

The Colorado courts determined that because Phillips rejected Scardina's message, he was discriminating against her transgender identity, so they ruled against him. The editors of the *National Review* suggest a double standard:

> Thus, a person's homosexual or transgender identity is discriminated against unless others endorse the person's conduct and views. This was the theory of those who demanded that the National Hockey League's Ivan Provorov publicly wear a Pride jersey. Yet, the *Christian* identity of Phillips or Provorov must give way when he seeks to put it into action, words, or even simple silence. The right of Christians to faith-based conduct and expression, or even the right of nonreligious people to remain true to themselves if that means differing in opinion on the nature of gender and sexual orientation, must be forcibly separated from their identity.
>
> The liberal promise of anti-discrimination laws is that they secure the same rights to all in a neutral fashion. The illiberal reality of their deployment by progressives in clashes between sex-based identity and faith-based identity is to demand that the faithful kneel before favored identity groups.[4]

Barronelle Stutzman

Jack Phillips was present on December 5, 2017, for the hearing of Washington state floral artist Barronelle Stutzman before the US Supreme Court. Stutzman had been a small-town florist, the owner of Arlene's Flowers, for thirty years. She had a client, Rob Ingersoll, with whom she'd been friends for a decade. She says, "I knew he was in a relationship with a man and he knew I was a Christian. But that never clouded the friendship for either of us or threatened our shared creativity—until he asked me to design something special to celebrate his upcoming wedding.…As a

Christian, weddings have a particular significance. Marriage does celebrate two people's love for one another, but its sacred meaning goes far beyond that. Surely without intending to do so, Rob was asking me to choose between my affection for him and my commitment to Christ. As deeply fond as I am of Rob, my relationship with Jesus is everything to me."[5]

Stutzman thought they had parted as friends, but after Ingersoll's partner posted the details on his Facebook page, the story spread to the media. The Washington state attorney general filed an "unprecedented" lawsuit against her, claiming that she was required by state law to either create custom floral art celebrating same-sex ceremonies or give up her wedding business. In 2013, the ACLU brought an anti-discrimination lawsuit against her on behalf of Ingersoll and his partner. And after that, she was beset by reporters, phone calls, hate mail, and even death threats.[6]

The case might still be in the courts except that late in 2021 Stutzman ended the eight-year battle by settling with Ingersoll and his husband for a $5,000 payment. The settlement enabled her to "preserve her conscience" by not compromising her beliefs and prevented her from having to pay "potentially ruinous attorneys' fees." But it also forced her into retirement. She said, "I am willing to turn the legal struggle for freedom over to others. At age 77, it's time to retire and give my business to someone else."[7]

Joe Kennedy

And as I write this, high school football coach Joe Kennedy has just resigned. He was fired in 2015 by the Bremerton (Washington) School District, who feared that his habit of public post-game prayers constituted endorsement of religion and violated the separation of church and state. Kennedy filed a lawsuit in August 2016 on the basis that the school district violated his First Amendment rights. What followed was a seven-year legal battle to get his job back, which was finally granted by the US

Supreme Court in June 2022. Yet after coaching his first game in the fall of 2023, he resigned, citing family health concerns in Florida and a desire to work outside the school system to advocate for constitutional freedom and religious liberty.[8]

An article I recently read cites the experiences of these three people to make a powerful argument:

> Despite what some may claim, Christians are being persecuted in America. That might be hard to hear, but it's true. Even though the United States is, arguably, the freest nation on the planet, and offers the First Amendment protection, Christians still face already-and-increasing persecution here between our shining seas. We need to recognize this and prepare for it to get worse....I've heard from Christians who know they are unlikely to ever get promoted past a certain point at major corporations and consulting firms for holding to their sexual ethics. What do you call it when a Christian is fired for believing that, according to God's Word, God made men as men and women as women and only those two genders? Or for refusing to tell lies by using she/her or they/them to describe he/him? It's persecution.[9]

The three people just cited have become public spectacles over the last decade. Meanwhile, untold other examples are popping up in businesses and communities across the nation with little fanfare. In some instances, Christians are being denied the right to pray publicly without facing legal consequences. In others, they are choosing to resign or be fired when faced with demands that they work on their Sabbath (whether Saturday or Sunday)— even when they demonstrate a willingness to compensate by working overtime or swapping schedules with other employees.

In a recent United Nations dialogue on intercultural and interreligious matters, held to discuss concern for recent religion-based problems, this was their summary statement:

There is a growing concern about the overall rise in instances of discrimination, intolerance and violence, regardless of the actors, directed against members of many religious, ethnic, and other communities in various parts of the world, including cases motivated by Islamophobia, antisemitism and Christianophobia and prejudices against persons of other religions or beliefs.[10]

THE ROOTS OF PERSECUTION

We are accustomed to hearing about Christian persecution in other countries. It's been a fact of life for more than two thousand years now. But isn't it still more than a little alarming to consider that "Christianophobia" might be gaining ground in the United States? Let's look at some reasons why that might be taking place.

Demographic Shifts and Cultural Fragmentation

The United States has experienced significant demographic changes over the years, with increasing cultural diversity and the rise of nonreligious affiliations. As the nation becomes more pluralistic, Christians may perceive themselves as a minority in certain regions, leading to a sense of insecurity and vulnerability. This in turn tends to amplify perceived threats and create tensions between different religious groups, potentially leading to acts of persecution against Christians.

Politicization of Religion

For over two centuries, the United States has been predominantly influenced by Judeo-Christian values, with the ideals of justice, equality, and morality deeply rooted in these traditions. The cultural fabric of the nation has been shaped by this heritage, and it has influenced political discourse and policy decisions. However, as the American population becomes increasingly diverse and interconnected, the need for representation and understanding of other faiths and belief systems becomes more apparent.

The blending of religion and politics has been a persistent aspect of American society, and in recent times this trend has intensified. The polarizing nature of politics often leads to the demonization of certain religious groups, now including Christians, by opponents seeking to mobilize their base. This politicization could foster an environment where Christians are targeted as "the other," leading to discrimination and, in extreme cases, persecution.

Political Polarization

Political polarization in America has spilled over into religious debates, where issues of morality and ethics often intersect with political stances. As politicians align themselves with certain religious or secular factions, it can further polarize public opinion on religious matters. This politicization of religion can exacerbate tensions between Christian values and secular ideologies, potentially leading to social divisions and discrimination.

Backlash From Extreme Elements

The actions of a few radicalized individuals or fringe groups who claim to represent any religion can have far-reaching and sometimes unintended consequences. When extremist elements with Christian roots misinterpret Scripture and commit violent acts or espouse hateful ideologies, they may provoke a backlash from other communities or governments. As a result, innocent Christians could face collective blame and suffer unjust persecution for the actions of a misguided minority.

Shifts in Legal Interpretations

American law has long upheld the principle of religious freedom and protected the rights of individuals to practice their faith without discrimination. However, shifts in legal interpretations and court decisions could potentially erode those protections. If the balance between religious freedom and other societal interests tilts unfavorably, it may open the door for targeted measures against Christian beliefs and practices.

The idea that rights are granted by a divine source has been a cornerstone of the American ethos since its inception. The Declaration of Independence famously declares that individuals are "endowed by their Creator with certain unalienable Rights." This assertion reflects a philosophical and theological perspective that forms the basis of the nation's fundamental freedoms.

The foundation of the American Constitution is also rooted in the belief that certain inalienable rights are endowed by a higher power, often referred to as "God." This concept has played a significant role in shaping the values and principles of the United States. However, as America undergoes a process of secularization, where religious influence is gradually diminishing in society, it is foreseeable that the traditional Judeo-Christian ideals underpinning the nation's framework could soon face challenges.

The presence of religious language in foundational documents has long been a topic of debate, as it raises questions about the relationship between religion and governance. Today there is a growing emphasis on the separation of religion from public institutions and policies. As religious diversity increases and the influence of organized religion wanes, the traditional Judeo-Christian perspective could be challenged by a more inclusive and pluralistic understanding of rights. Secularization encourages a broader perspective on the sources of human rights, focusing on principles of reason, ethics, and humanity rather than relying solely on religious doctrine.

As America becomes more diverse and interconnected, the role of religion in shaping public policy and governance may very well lead to various levels of persecution for Christians.

Social and Cultural Changes

Changing social attitudes can significantly impact the perception of Christianity in America. The growth of secularism and the increasing acceptance of progressive ideologies are likely to lead to conflicts with traditional Christian values. In such a climate, Christians may be deemed intolerant or out of touch with contemporary norms, making them susceptible to social ostracizing and ultimately persecution.

A shifting social outlook can also play a crucial role in determining how various religious groups are perceived and treated within a society. Consider some of the current ongoing social shifts:

- *Increasing secularism.* In recent decades, we've seen a noticeable decline in religious affiliation and practice across the United States. This trend of secularism, where individuals identify as nonreligious or have weak religious ties, has led to a decrease in the influence of religious institutions in shaping societal norms. As religious practices and beliefs become less prevalent, traditional Christian values may face opposition or be considered outdated by segments of the population.

- *Acceptance of progressive ideologies.* The acceptance of progressive ideologies (such as gender equality, LGBTQ+ rights, and reproductive freedom) has increasingly become a hallmark of modern American society. These values often clash with certain conservative Christian beliefs, particularly on issues related to sexuality and family structures. As a result, Christians who adhere to traditional teachings may be viewed as intolerant or discriminatory, even if their intention is to uphold their religious convictions and even if they remain nonjudgmental toward others.

- *Altered cultural perception.* The media and entertainment industries have a powerful impact on how religious groups are portrayed and perceived by the general public. In recent years, we've seen a growing trend of critiquing or satirizing Christianity in various forms of media, contributing to the perception that Christian beliefs are at odds with contemporary cultural norms. Such representations can reinforce stereotypes and contribute to the marginalization of Christians, fostering a climate of social ostracizing.

Misunderstandings and Stereotypes

In any diverse society, misunderstandings and stereotypes can arise between different religious groups. Misinformation about Christianity, whether intentional or not, can fuel misconceptions and negative perceptions. For example, some individuals may associate Christianity with certain historical events or actions taken by specific Christian groups, leading to generalized negative attitudes toward all Christians.

Marginalization of Conservative Christianity

In some academic and intellectual circles, conservative Christianity is often viewed with suspicion or dismissed as incompatible with modern thought. This marginalization can influence public discourse and policy making, resulting in limited recognition of Christian perspectives and concerns.

Legal Challenges

In recent years conflicts between religious freedoms and anti-discrimination laws have emerged in various contexts. Christian business owners and organizations have faced legal challenges when their beliefs clashed with prevailing laws, especially regarding issues such as same-sex marriage and gender identity. Such legal disputes can contribute to the perception of Christians as resistant to societal progress and result in negative social consequences.

External Influences

International events and global politics can also influence attitudes toward religious groups within America. Acts of terrorism or violent conflicts involving religious extremist groups overseas may fuel anti-Christian sentiment at home. This could lead to the unjust scapegoating of American Christians and contribute to a climate of persecution.

Online Disinformation and Echo Chambers

Misinformation and the presence of echo chambers on social media platforms can contribute to the vilification of religious groups, including Christians. False narratives and malicious propaganda can fuel hatred and distrust, leading to potential discrimination and persecution in real-world settings.

PERSECUTION AS A POSITIVE SIGN?

The United States has long been blessed with freedoms that are rare, if not unheard of, in other parts of the world. From America's onset, freedom of religion was written into our founding documents and legal systems. Christianity has been the dominant religion for centuries, but that doesn't mean it hasn't created problems at times. The well-intentioned efforts of European-American Christians to evangelize indigenous peoples sometimes did more harm than good as missionaries attempted to change not only spiritual understanding but language, dress, and culture as well. Most recent efforts have more respect for native tribes and other cultures, yet soured memories remain.

As we learn to accept criticism when it is deserved, the modern church can then learn from past mistakes and do a better job of connecting with nonbelievers who are open to hearing about the love and grace of God and the sacrifice of Jesus Christ.

Other times, however, we will receive criticism—and maybe even persecution—that we don't deserve. When we do, we shouldn't be surprised. Jesus told us not only to expect it, but to try to appreciate it! In His Sermon on the Mount, He summarized the Beatitudes with this reminder: "Blessed are you when they revile and persecute you, and say all kinds of evil against you falsely for My sake. Rejoice and be exceedingly glad, for great is your reward in heaven, for so they persecuted the prophets who were before you" (Matt. 5:11–12).

Jesus' followers saw the opposition, criticism, and persecution He received from others during His three years of ministry. And shortly before He returned to the Father, He cautioned them to expect criticism:

> If the world hates you, you know that it hated Me before it hated you. If you were of the world, the world would love its own. Yet because you are not of the world, but I chose you out of the world, therefore the world hates you. Remember the word that I said to you, "A servant is not greater than his master." If they persecuted Me, they will also persecute you. If they kept My word, they will keep yours also. But all these things they will do to you for My name's sake, because they do not know Him who sent Me.
>
> —John 15:18–21

Perhaps then if we in America are beginning to experience persecution, maybe it's because we're doing something right. If we take a stand against misinformation, clarify half-truths, and hold fast to the teachings of the Scriptures, we're likely to become targets. Maybe many in the church haven't felt persecuted because they've become complacent. It's easy enough to divert your eyes and walk the other way whenever you see or hear an offense against God and/or a fellow believer. It's not difficult to downplay your personal beliefs in today's culture if you find yourself among a group of people who vehemently oppose "judgmental" Christians who still believe some things are right and others are morally wrong, even if they've been legalized.

But the increasing number of people willing to sidestep confrontation to avoid persecution only makes it harder on the ones who faithfully take a stand against the burgeoning spiritual chaos in our culture. And we should never forget that those who stand for their Lord now can be confident that He will stand for them later—when it really matters (Matt. 10:33).

Chapter 12

Preparing for the Worst— or Only Prepping?

EOPLE OFTEN DISCUSS the last days and the end times, as well they should. Jesus and the Old Testament prophets have given us signs to watch for, many of which seem to be taking place before our eyes here and now. But in all those speculative discussions, we may be asking the wrong questions. If the world learned anything from the COVID crisis, perhaps it's that when we see a threatening situation approaching, the first question we need to ask is *not* "Are we sure we have enough toilet paper?"

You probably remember the Great Toilet Paper Crisis of 2020, perhaps one of the most emblematic episodes of the early days of the pandemic. Toilet paper, a humble household staple, suddenly became a hot commodity as people stockpiled rolls, fearing an indefinite shortage. Supermarket aisles were emptied, and nightly news images of barren shelves became a symbol of the general state of panic. The supply chains for toilet paper were largely unaffected, yet the purchasing frenzy was a manifestation of the human need for control in an uncontrollable situation.

Close on the heels of the toilet paper phenomenon was the rush for hand sanitizers, disinfectant sprays, and wipes. While personal hygiene and cleanliness were undeniably essential in preventing the spread of the virus, the demand far outpaced the supply. Bottles of hand sanitizers were being sold at exorbitant prices online, and many households hoarded more disinfectant than they could possibly use in years. This panic buying made it difficult for everyone, especially frontline workers, to access those essential items.

Simultaneously came a surge in purchases of nonperishable food items. Pasta, rice, canned goods, and flour saw a massive spike in sales. Many households, responding to fears of a long-term lockdown or supply chain disruptions, began stockpiling such goods.

Then, due to lockdowns and/or shelter-in-place restrictions, the panic buying and other spending expanded beyond the essentials. With more time confined indoors, people purchased various items to combat boredom and create a "new normal." Sales of fitness equipment, home office furniture, and even puzzles skyrocketed.

Meanwhile, the pandemic continued to run its course. Every day we saw the latest grim statistics and the stress mounting for health care workers and first responders. In many cases our hoarding only made things worse, but at least we were doing *something*. The pandemic unveiled a myriad of global challenges, from health care crises to economic downturns. Still, on a more micro level, the sudden rush to buy unnecessary goods offered a unique window into human behavior in the face of unprecedented challenges. While it's easy to view some of these purchases as irrational, retrospectively, they underscore the collective human need for control, security, and a semblance of normalcy in turbulent times.

So it seems the first question we need to ask ourselves as we look to the future and fear what may be here sooner than we're expecting is "How *do* I prepare for midnight? How do I prepare for the chaos that Jesus and the prophets warned us about?"

UNDERSTANDING THE PANIC

Consider what led to the surge in panic buying during the pandemic. At its core, this behavior can be attributed to the human psyche trying to establish a sense of control in a situation over which we have no control. I see the issue as a difference between *prepping*, which I define as a spontaneous, hands-on response to the crisis, and true *preparation*, which requires stepping back to calmly and rationally assess the situation at hand.

For example, you might prep for a medical procedure. That would likely require you to fast for twenty-four hours before any kind of surgery, or take special medicine. You might need to allow a nurse attendant to shave the area to be treated. But after you, and perhaps others, do all *you* can do, you must still put your future into the hands of a doctor who will be primarily responsible for the outcome. Wise people put much effort into finding a doctor they trust for such a responsibility.

Prepping is rooted in the tangible fears of our age. Whether it's concern over natural disasters, financial collapses, or pandemics, individuals find solace in knowing they've done *something* to prepare themselves. This modern movement prompts individuals to stockpile food, water, and other necessities, ensuring they can survive should the worst happen. Prepping, in this sense, is an insurance policy against unpredictability, a hedge against the unknown.

When the COVID pandemic first hit the global scene, an unexpected and overwhelming wave of panic swept across communities worldwide. A sense of impending doom, combined with the uncertainty surrounding the virus, catalyzed a series of reactions that few could have anticipated. Among the most vivid illustrations of this collective anxiety was the sudden and inexplicable rush to purchase, often in bulk, a myriad of goods—many of which, upon reflection, seemed unnecessary.

It certainly gets a bit ridiculous when your best response to a pandemic is a knee-jerk reaction like stocking up on toilet paper. But in their defense, other preppers invest time, money, and effort into building sustainable systems for food and water. They learn agricultural skills, invest in water purification methods, and often create long-term storage solutions. The underlying principle is simple: when trouble comes, those who are prepared have the best chance of survival.

The rise of global uncertainties has sparked an interest in preparing for potential future disasters across all levels of society. At its core, prepping revolves around the collection of essential resources, with food and water being paramount. Yet when we explore the teachings of Christianity, a different perspective on preparedness emerges.

A Better Option

In stark contrast to the modern, pragmatic prepping movement stands the Sermon on the Mount, one of the most celebrated teachings of Jesus Christ. In the Gospel of Matthew (chapters 5–7), Jesus imparts wisdom that calls for a different level of preparedness.

When approaching any uncertain situation, the practical, worldly response of prepping may seem like quite a contradiction to the ongoing spiritual readiness Jesus emphasizes in the Sermon on the Mount, yet they may have more alignment than you think. Just as you take practical steps to prep for surgery, while remembering that your reliance on your surgeon is far more important, we can prep for potential disasters in life while learning to live in total dependence on God and the wisdom He provides to guide us through the worst that humankind and Satan can throw at us.

The primary difference between being prepared, as the Sermon on the Mount suggests, and prepping in a worldly sense lies in the object of our trust. Our trust must be in God alone and not in our ability. Let's take a closer look at the Sermon on the Mount as a spiritual blueprint:

> Therefore I say to you, do not worry about your life, what you will eat or what you will drink; nor about your body, what you will put on. Is not life more than food and the body more than clothing? Look at the birds of the air, for they neither sow nor reap nor gather into barns; yet your heavenly Father feeds them. Are you not of more value than they? Which of you by worrying can add one cubit to his stature?
>
> So why do you worry about clothing? Consider the lilies of the field, how they grow: they neither toil nor spin; and yet I say to you that even Solomon in all his glory was not arrayed like one of these. Now if God so clothes the grass of the field, which today is, and tomorrow is thrown into the oven, will He not much more clothe you, O you of little faith?
>
> Therefore do not worry, saying, "What shall we eat?" or "What shall we drink?" or "What shall we wear?" For after all these things the Gentiles seek. For your heavenly Father knows that you need all these things. But seek first the kingdom of God and His righteousness, and all these things shall be added to you. Therefore do not worry about tomorrow, for tomorrow will worry about its own things. Sufficient for the day is its own trouble.
>
> —Matthew 6:25–34

Jesus challenges us not to worry so much about food or clothing. This suggests a radical shift from our natural instincts. Instead of focusing on material provisions, Christ points to the value of *spiritual* sustenance. He reminds us to look at the birds as an example of how God takes care of even the most fragile of His creation. His message is clear: have faith that God will provide. In this paradigm, spiritual readiness supersedes physical readiness. While prepping focuses on the tangibles, the Sermon on the Mount emphasizes intangibles such as faith and trust in God.

Prepping is largely a personal endeavor, one that empowers individuals to control their destinies to the best of their abilities. It's about ensuring self-reliance, taking matters into one's own hands, and preparing for a range of scenarios. Conversely, the kind of preparedness highlighted in the Sermon on the Mount leans heavily on divine providence. It's about cultivating a deep-seated trust that, regardless of the circumstances, God can and will provide and guide in the most challenging difficulties.

These two paradigms are not necessarily an either/or choice to make. They may sometimes seem at odds, yet they can coexist. One can argue that the act of prepping is a God-given instinct to preserve life, akin to the way animals store food for winter. Likewise, maintaining spiritual wellness and trust in divine providence does not negate the responsibility of ensuring the safety and well-being of one's family.

Being pragmatic doesn't have to compromise faith, and relying on God doesn't mean being passive or unprepared in a physical sense. Consider a balance that allows you to be at peace that you have done all you can do, but ultimately you have a faith that is anchored in the solid rock of God's power and truth. When the Israelites stood staring in fear at the Red Sea before them and the pursuing Egyptian army behind them, God told Moses, "Why do you cry to Me? Tell the children of Israel to go forward. But lift up your rod, and stretch out your hand over the sea and divide it. And the children of Israel shall go on dry ground through the midst of the sea" (Exod. 14:15–16). God was in control of the situation, but the people had their part to play in getting safely to the other side.

It's that personal change of perspective—to begin to see world events the way God sees them, rather than through our instinctive fear and foreboding—that makes all the difference. Few figures have made more of a dramatic change in perspective than St. Francis of Assisi. Born into a wealthy family of silk merchants in the late twelfth century, Francis enjoyed the luxuries of his privileged upbringing. However, a series of encounters, including a stint as a prisoner of war and a profound spiritual experience in the ruined church of San Damiano, led him to renounce his family's wealth. This dramatic renunciation was not merely about abandoning material riches; it signified a profound shift in priorities. Francis chose to place his entire trust in God's provision rather than the fleeting securities of the world.

Although he has become a romanticized image of a gentle friar preaching to birds or befriending wolves, Francis led a life that encapsulated a radical trust in God that few have emulated. His complete dependence on divine providence serves as a timeless model of faith and surrender. His profound connection with nature also underscored his trust in God. He viewed all creation as a testament to God's sustaining power and benevolence. By appreciating the lilies of the field and the birds of the air, Francis lived Jesus' teaching in the Sermon on the Mount about God's care for humankind and all of creation.

A PRACTICAL AND EFFECTIVE PLAN OF PREPAREDNESS

As we move through the complex tapestry of life, the concept of the "end times" is an underlying concern for many, influenced by both religious teachings and global events. While there are various interpretations of what this means, one common theme emerges: the need for preparedness, both physical and spiritual. The question then becomes: How does one prepare for unforeseeable events while maintaining unwavering faith in God? In our efforts to trust our futures to God more wholeheartedly, what should we be doing in the meantime?

Understanding biblical teachings

To begin with, it's essential to have a clear understanding of what the Bible says about the end of times. In Christian theology, the Book of Revelation provides detailed imagery of what the end times may look like. While it's open to various interpretations, one takeaway is certain: the importance of remaining steadfast in faith. When you understand your faith's perspective on the matter, it allows you to navigate the road ahead with clarity and purpose.

Preparing spiritually

Before delving into physical preparations, your spiritual readiness is paramount. This involves several crucial aspects of spiritual commitment.

Praying

Like any relationship, your bond with God grows stronger with regular communication. Prayer offers solace, guidance, and an opportunity to seek wisdom through:

- *Staying consistent*—Just as the body requires daily sustenance, the soul thrives on consistent spiritual nourishment. Regular prayer ensures that the heart remains attuned to God's voice.

- *Seeking and surrendering*—Prayer is a dual act of seeking and surrendering. While it's a space to present one's desires, anxieties, and needs, it is also a realm of surrender, of recognizing God's sovereignty and embracing His will.

- *Being anchored*—From personal setbacks to global crises, life's challenges can be overwhelming. Regular prayer offers an anchor, grounding you in the presence of God and His Word.

Studying the Bible

Regularly reading and studying the Bible provides insights into God's promises and instructions for living a righteous life, especially during challenging times. The Bible, often referred to as God's Word, offers a wealth of wisdom, guidance, and solace. Regularly immersing oneself in its teachings equips and prepares you to navigate life's complexities.

- *Discovering timeless truths*—Every page of the Bible contains timeless truths. Whether it's the lessons of biblical history, the Psalms' poetic expressions of human emotions, the Proverbs' nuggets of wisdom, the insightful revelation of the Prophets, Jesus' challenging parables and teachings, or the fundamental doctrines throughout the apostle Paul's letters, Scripture contains a reservoir of insights awaiting discovery.

- *Equipping for challenges*—The Bible is filled with stories of ordinary individuals confronting extraordinary challenges, from Moses facing Pharaoh, to David standing up to Goliath, to Esther advocating for her people. Studying these narratives offers both encouragement and practical lessons for facing modern challenges.

- *Affirming God's promises*—The Scriptures are filled with divine promises, assurances of God's presence, provision, and protection. Regular study reinforces these promises, embedding them deep within the heart and providing hope in trying times.

While the Scriptures indeed provide assurances of God's presence, provision, and protection, the promise of Christ's return amplifies these assurances manifold. It reinforces hope, reshapes perspectives, and reminds believers of God's redemptive plan.

Engaging the community

Engaging with a faith-based community can provide support, shared resources, and diverse perspectives on interpreting and handling challenges. While personal spiritual practices are indispensable, we find unparalleled strength in collective faith. In challenging times, communities become even more crucial. Engaging with a faith-based community extends several benefits.

- *Shared resources*—Within a community, both spiritual and material resources often come to light. They can range from collective prayers and intercession to pooling together physical resources in times of need. The early Christians sold their possessions to ensure everyone's needs were met (Acts 2:44–45). This spirit of collective well-being is an essential aspect of navigating crises.

- *Diverse perspectives*—A community invariably consists of individuals from varied backgrounds, each bringing a unique perspective. Engaging in discussions, working through Bible studies, or simply sharing life experiences can provide fresh insights and broaden everyone's understanding of faith and life.

- *Mutual support*—Knowing there's a community to lean on can be immensely reassuring during a challenging phase, a personal crisis, or a global event. Whether it's sharing skills or simply offering emotional support, strong community ties can make a significant difference.

Preparing physically

With a strong spiritual foundation, you can then address the practical aspects of preparation.

- *Stockpiling essentials*—Ensure you have nonperishable food, clean water, medical supplies, and other necessities. Remember, the purpose isn't to hoard what you need but to ensure you and your loved ones have adequate supplies for potential emergencies.

- *Learning skills*—Acquire skills such as gardening, basic first aid, and water purification can be invaluable. As you become more self-reliant, you can then share with your community, reflecting the biblical principles of being a good Samaritan and treating others as you would like to be treated.

- *Staying informed*—Maintain ongoing awareness of global events, and understand potential threats when making informed decisions about preparedness. However, it's vital to filter information to avoid unnecessary panic and misinformation. During the early days of the COVID lockdown, the mainstream news networks were all following the same narrative: "Trust the science." It made sense at that time—until it didn't. Before long, a lot of questionable theories and unproven recommendations began to circulate. In January 2021 I was one of a group of committed people who launched AmericanFaith.com to provide "News You Can Trust." After such a period of rampant misinformation and biased reporting, we wanted to provide the American people with a news media outlet that embraced journalistic integrity. The platform now stands as a beacon of verified, reliable news. Every story undergoes rigorous fact-checking, ensuring that readers receive not just *timely* but also *accurate* information.

Embracing trust in God

Even as you do all you can to prepare for what's to come, it's essential to strike a balance between self-reliance and trust in God. The Bible reminds us to "Trust in the Lord with all your heart, and lean not on your own understanding; in all your ways acknowledge Him, and He shall direct your paths" (Prov. 3:5–6). This suggests that while we should take practical action, our trust should ultimately rest in God's plan.

1. Nurture mental and emotional well-being. End-times prophecies or worldly challenges can take a toll on mental health. It's crucial to recognize this and ensure that you're nurturing your emotional well-being. This might involve seeking counseling, engaging in meditative practices, or simply having open conversations with loved ones about fears and concerns.

2. Reevaluate and adapt. As with any form of preparedness, regular reevaluation is essential. As situations evolve, your approach to preparedness should adapt. This applies to both physical resources and spiritual understanding and growth.

A philosophy often attributed to St. Augustine suggests one should "Pray as though everything depends on God and work as if everything depends on you." The merging of unwavering trust in God and human preparedness can seem complex, but it boils down to a simple principle: while we do what we can to prep on earth, our ultimate trust lies in the divine. Balancing our commonsense preparations for the end times with strong and steady faith in God requires understanding that we have a dual role to play. We are to be individuals of action, equipped with the skills and resources to face challenges, *and* individuals of faith, relying on God for guidance and sustenance. As we walk this path of preparation, let it be a journey that deepens our faith, enriches our spirit, and equips us for whatever the future holds.

BACK TO THE SERMON ON THE MOUNT

At its core, the Sermon on the Mount offers not only ethical instructions but also deep insights into the nature of God's care and the human inclination toward worry. One of its many timeless teachings is an exhortation to trust in God's providence.

God's providence and provision

We saw that in the Sermon on the Mount, Jesus encourages His followers not to worry about the future, asserting that God, who takes care of the birds and the lilies, will surely care for His people! Jesus uses the metaphor of nature—birds and flowers—to deliver a poignant message about trust (Matt. 6:26). He emphasizes the importance of trust in God's provision and warns against excessive anxiety about the future.

The imagery is vivid. Birds, without the ability to store food, rely on the daily provisions of nature, and they thrive. The lilies, "which neither toil nor spin," are arrayed in splendor surpassing even Solomon's glory (Matt. 6:28–29). Through these examples, Jesus underscores a simple yet profound truth: If God cares for the lesser creatures and flowers, how much more would He care for human beings, the pinnacle of His creation?

The futility of worry

Further into the discourse, Jesus asks, "And which of you by worrying can add one cubit to his stature?" (Matt. 6:27). Other translations interpret His question to be, "Which of you by worrying can add a single day to his lifespan?" Either way, this rhetorical question underscores the futility of excessive worry. Anxiety doesn't change our circumstances. It doesn't improve us physically or extend our lives. If anything, undue stress both creates health problems and hinders our ability to appreciate God's provisions in every moment of each new day.

A matter of priority

Jesus then offers a solution to our human propensity to worry: "But seek first the kingdom of God and His righteousness, and all these things shall be added to you" (Matt. 6:33). Instead of becoming ensnared in the anxieties of worldly needs and desires, Jesus invites His followers to redirect their focus. By prioritizing the pursuit of God's kingdom and His righteousness, believers are assured that their needs—whether physical, emotional, or spiritual—will be met.

Embracing the present

Following this counsel, Jesus delivers one of His most quoted teachings: "Therefore do not worry about tomorrow, for tomorrow will worry about its own things. Sufficient for the day is its own trouble" (Matt. 6:34). In other words, every day has plenty of trouble on its own; no need to be worrying in advance! It's a call to mindfulness, a reminder that while planning for the future has its place, excessive preoccupation with the uncertainties of tomorrow can rob you of the joys and lessons of today. Each day, both challenges and blessings provide new opportunities for growth, faith, and deeper reliance on God.

A greater commitment to trust

The teachings from the Sermon on the Mount offer more than just guidelines—they provide a worldview. They present a God who is intimately involved in the well-being of His creation. He is not a distant, indifferent deity but a loving Father who knows our needs even before we voice them.

To trust in such divine providence, as Jesus teaches, we must refuse to settle for passivity or negligence but instead cultivate a heart that recognizes God's omnipotence and benevolence. We must learn to move through life with the conviction that, even in the face of great challenges and difficulties, God's purposes are at work and His provisions are sure. God calls us to anchor our lives not in the transient and unpredictable but in the eternal and unchanging love of God. In doing so, we find not only peace amid storms but also the strength to navigate them, assured of God's unwavering care.

OTHER BIBLICAL MOTIVATIONS

The Sermon on the Mount is a classic passage to inspire us to ponder and perhaps reconsider our actions concerning our faith, but there are others. Our faith draws on a rich tapestry of teachings, narratives, and interpretations, including the idea of prepping and preparing for potential future disasters—not least among them the concept of the end times.

The Bible, particularly in the New Testament, provides warnings about challenging times. Revelation, for instance, contains symbolic descriptions of events leading up to the end of the world. Similarly, in the Gospels Jesus occasionally spoke of tribulations. Given these teachings, it would seem prudent for believers to be aware and as prepared as possible to face adversities. Throughout the Bible, wisdom and prudence are extolled as virtues. For example, "A prudent man foresees evil and hides himself, but the simple pass on and are punished" (Prov. 22:3). From this perspective, preparing for potential threats could be viewed as a wise and prudent action, aligned with biblical teachings.

However, at the same time, the Bible also cautions against living in fear. Second Timothy 1:7 notes, "For God has not given us a spirit of fear, but of power and of love and of a sound mind." If the motivation behind prepping is sheer panic or distrust in God's providence, there might be a conflict with the Christian call to trust in God's care. Preparation should not become an obsession that eclipses one's faith and trust in divine providence.

The New Testament is rich with parables that convey profound spiritual truths. Among these, the parable of the ten virgins (Matt. 25:1–13) stands out as a reminder of the significance of spiritual vigilance and the importance of being prepared for the unknown:

> Then the kingdom of heaven shall be likened to ten virgins who took their lamps and went out to meet the bridegroom. Now five of them were wise, and five were foolish. Those who were foolish took their lamps and took no oil with them, but the wise took oil in their vessels with their lamps. But while the bridegroom was delayed, they all slumbered and slept.
>
> And at midnight a cry was heard: "Behold, the bridegroom is coming; go out to meet him!" Then all those virgins arose and trimmed their lamps. And the foolish said to the wise, "Give us some of your oil, for our lamps are going out." But the wise answered, saying, "No, lest there should not be enough for us and you; but go rather to those who sell, and buy for yourselves." And while they went to buy, the

bridegroom came, and those who were ready went in with him to the wedding; and the door was shut.

Afterward the other virgins came also, saying, "Lord, Lord, open to us!" But he answered and said, "Assuredly, I say to you, I do not know you."

Watch therefore, for you know neither the day nor the hour in which the Son of Man is coming.

—MATTHEW 25:1–13

At its surface, this parable presents a simple scenario—ten virgins awaiting the arrival of the bridegroom. Yet as the narrative unfolds, the contrasting behaviors of the virgins offer profound insights. Half of them were wise and brought extra oil for their lamps, while the others did not. This parable, while primarily emphasizing spiritual preparedness, also underscores the value of foresight and readiness. When the bridegroom (representing Christ) came, only those who were prepared could join Him.

The symbolism of oil in the parable is a crucial element—it determines the readiness of the virgins. The oil represents the Holy Spirit. Just as lamps without oil cannot produce light, so a soul without spiritual sustenance cannot truly shine in God's presence. The wise virgins are characterized by their foresight in bringing extra oil, ensuring their lamps remain lit. Conversely, the foolish virgins, having failed to anticipate the bridegroom's delay, find themselves unprepared when he finally arrives.

The bridegroom's unexpected delay is a critical element of the parable. It mirrors the unpredictability of Christ's second coming, a central theme in Christian eschatology. Believers are repeatedly reminded throughout the New Testament to be watchful, because the exact time of His return remains unknown. The delay serves as a test of the virgins' readiness, revealing their true preparedness.

After the wise virgins enter the feast, a stark reality confronts the foolish virgins—the bridegroom will not recognize them. The closed door symbolizes the finality of God's judgment, stressing the importance of spiritual vigilance in the present. Once the moment passes, opportunities for redemption might be lost.

The parable concludes with a universal call to vigilance: "Watch therefore, for you know neither the day nor the hour" (Matt. 25:13). This emphasis on watchfulness echoes Christ's consistent message throughout the Gospels, urging believers to live in a state of readiness, not lulled into complacency by the routines and distractions of daily life.

Beyond its eschatological implications, the parable of the ten virgins offers practical lessons for daily Christian living:

- *Spiritual nourishment*—Just as the wise virgins ensured their lamps were well-supplied, believers are encouraged to continually nourish their spiritual lives through prayer, Scripture study, and communion with God.

- *Vigilance in faith*—The Christian journey is marked by constant watchfulness—against temptations, against complacency, and for opportunities to serve and grow in faith.

- *Anticipating Christ's presence*—While the parable hints at Christ's second coming, it also reminds believers to recognize and welcome His presence in their daily lives, being always ready to encounter Him.

What emerges from these biblical reflections is a call for balance. On one hand, Christians are encouraged to trust in God's provision, and on the other they are reminded of the virtues of prudence and preparation. The key lies in the motivation and attitude toward prepping:

- If prepping springs from a place of wisdom and a desire to care for one's family and community, it aligns with the Christian values of stewardship and responsibility.

- If, however, prepping stems from a place of consuming fear, paranoia, or lack of trust in God's provision, it may be worth reevaluating one's approach and seeking spiritual guidance.

In essence, Christianity does not specifically condemn the act of preparing for future uncertainties. As with many things in life, it's not the action but the intention of the heart that matter most. Christians considering prepping should examine their motivations and ensure they're rooted in love, responsibility, and prudence rather than fear or distrust. Engaging in prayer, seeking counsel from spiritual leaders, and immersing themselves in biblical teachings can provide clarity on this path.

In a world filled with uncertainties, the Christian journey involves navigating between trusting in God's providence and exercising the wisdom He bestows. By keeping faith at the forefront and ensuring actions align with Christian principles, believers can confidently tread the path of preparedness without compromising their spiritual integrity.

PART IV: A LOOK WITHIN

WHEN YOU OPEN your eyes to what may seem to be the ever-deteriorating state of our nation and the world, what *should* be your response? Instinctively, many of us are quickly consumed by fear, dread, and other unhelpful emotions. Those are natural responses to grim and disheartening news, but they are also tools of the enemy.

The reason God's Word is so specific about what to expect is for believers to prepare for whatever comes. The Book of Revelation has some of the most frightening images of anywhere in Scripture, yet it was written for the church with repeated promises offered to those who "overcome." The purpose of knowing what's to come, along with an unfiltered awareness of what's taking place around us, is so we can ready ourselves for any conflict, physical or spiritual.

We're closing with this section, which is a challenge to create a *mindset* that God is always in control. It's a final reminder that you are never outside of His protective care, no matter what happens. If you are troubled by all the things you're seeing, you need only to change your focus. Believers are challenged to "set your mind on things above, not on things on the earth" (Col. 3:2). Let's now see how you can do that.

Chapter 13

Fear Is a Spirit

FOR A BRIEF stint, my family and I resided in England as I pursued my studies at Oxford University. This afforded us the unique opportunity to explore various European cities. On one sightseeing expedition, we found ourselves arriving in Prague, Czech Republic, shortly after midnight. I was walking with my wife and twelve-year-old daughter, passing through a dimly lit tunnel leading from the train station, when a sense of dread overcame me. It was more than the feeling of being disoriented in a new city; it was spiritual. My wife and daughter voiced similar feelings of fear at the same moment.

How do you navigate situations like that? Though I sensed the fear as vividly as my family did, societal expectations as the "man of the house" compelled me to mask my personal anxiety. I tried to reassure them: "We're fine; it's all good." Yet a part of me was convinced that something evil was lurking in that tunnel, as though the very atmosphere was saturated with a spirit of fear. By the grace of God, we safely exited the tunnel and hailed a taxi to our hotel.

That unnerving experience often resurfaces in my memory, serving as a reminder of the spiritual realm that interweaves with our natural world. We inhabit a reality where spiritual battles occur ceaselessly, many escaping our notice. To "see" these spiritual battles, our eyes need to be opened to the realm beyond our five senses.

Unseen Enemies, Unseen Help

According to the Bible, ministering angels surround us to offer support, even as demonic forces scheme toward our downfall. To prevail in this spiritual warfare, it's imperative to immerse ourselves in the teachings of the Scriptures and acknowledge the spiritual landscapes we tread upon.

One emphatic example of such spiritual battles was recounted in the autobiography of John G. Paton, a nineteenth-century Scottish missionary. He traveled to the New Hebrides Islands in the South Pacific, now known as the Solomon Islands, to work and teach among the people there. At the time, the indigenous population practiced cannibalism and had historically been resistant to Christian teachings.

Upon Paton's arrival, he was met with suspicion, hostility, and even threats of violence. His mission seemed doomed from the outset, a fool's errand in the eyes of many back home. But Paton firmly believed in the protective circle of ministering angels spoken of in the Bible, and he set about his work with an unshakeable resolve.

One fascinating story recounts a night when Paton was surrounded by hostile tribesmen intent on burning down the mission and killing its inhabitants. All seemed lost; there appeared to be no way out. Paton and his wife spent the entire tense night in prayer. When dawn broke, they found that the tribesmen had retreated. Years later, Paton discovered from one of the tribal chiefs that the natives had been frightened away by what appeared to be an army of large, shining men encircling the mission compound. Here perhaps was a real-world manifestation of angels, as mentioned in Hebrews 1:14: "Are [angels] not all ministering spirits sent forth to minister for those who will inherit salvation?"[1]

Paton's life vividly exemplifies how one might draw upon spiritual resources to navigate both external and internal challenges. He immersed himself deeply in the Scriptures as his source of faith. We would do well to be reminded that "faith comes by hearing, and hearing by the word of God" (Rom. 10:17).

The Word of God was Paton's compass in the treacherous spiritual landscapes he found himself in, landscapes where the forces of light and darkness were in stark contest. Although he faced dangers that were far more overt and immediate than my eerie tunnel experience in Prague, both were underscored by the same clash of spiritual realms. Both echo the same reality. We are players, whether we know it or not, in a constant cosmic drama, a spiritual struggle that unfolds daily:

> We do not wrestle against flesh and blood, but against principalities, against powers, against the rulers of the darkness of this age, against spiritual hosts of wickedness in the heavenly places. Therefore, take up the whole armor of God, that you may be able to withstand in the evil day, and having done all, to stand.
>
> —EPHESIANS 6:12–13

It's critical, especially in times when fear seems pervasive—be it during pandemics, societal upheavals, or personal crises—to lean on the strength and wisdom found in the Scriptures. Just as John Paton relied on his belief in divine protection, we too can find solace and courage through our faith, fortified by the knowledge that we are not alone in our spiritual journeys.

When Spiritual Eyes Are Opened

Angels are mentioned throughout the Bible in various roles and settings. But one of the best examples of them coming to the aid of God's people occurs during the ministry of the prophet Elisha. Israel was at war with Syria at the time. The king of Syria would pick a strategic place to set up camp to attack, but God would alert Elisha to his location, and the prophet would relate that information to the king of Israel. This happened time and time again until the king of Syria was convinced he had a mole among his ranks. But his officers told him, "Elisha, the prophet who is in Israel, tells the king of Israel the words that you speak in your bedroom" (2 Kings 6:12–17).

So the king of Syria made the capture of Elisha his top priority. He found out where Elisha was staying and sent "horses and chariots and a great army" (v. 14) during the night to surround the city. Elisha had a young servant with him who looked out the next morning and saw the surrounding hills filled with Syrian soldiers, horses, and chariots. He immediately warned Elisha of the danger and asked: "Alas, my master! What shall we do?" (v. 15).

Elisha wasn't bothered a bit. He assured his servant, "Do not fear, for those who are with us are more than those who are with them" (v. 16). Then Elijah prayed, "Lord, I pray, open his eyes that he may see" (v. 17). The next time the servant looked out, he didn't notice the Syrian army. All he could see was the mountain filled with horses and chariots of fire, a divine army far outmatching the Syrian forces. And when the Syrians started moving in, Elisha prayed again, "Strike this people, I pray, with blindness" (v. 18). Then Elisha walked out to the blinded army, told them to follow him, and said he would take them to the man they were seeking. But he led them into the city and right up to the Israelite king where he prayed again, this time for their sight to be restored.

Imagine their surprise when their sight returned and they saw they were surrounded and helpless. Elisha vetoed Israel's king's suggestion to kill them all. In a surprising act of grace, he instead served them a meal and sent them home. Wisely, the Syrians ceased their raids on Israel (2 Kings 6:8–23).

Elisha's response sets him apart as someone deeply in tune with the spiritual realm. He understood something his servant was yet to learn. He was operating on a different level than most people. Because Elisha's deep relationship with God had given him insight and revelation into the unseen world, he could exercise his faith in a way that fear could not affect.

You might wonder, "Is it possible for me to exercise my faith on this level?" The answer is yes! With each step of faith you are deepening your walk with God and enlarging your capacity to see and hear from Him. Adapt Elisha's prayer, and ask God to open your eyes to the spiritual world around you. It can greatly improve your perspective.

This struggle against fear was amplified globally during the COVID-19 pandemic. Unexpectedly, people I had considered unwavering in their faith capitulated to an atmosphere of fear. Many of them have not returned to their church or their faith.

TARES IN THE FABRIC OF SOCIETY

The falling away of so many people in the church may be partially explained in Jesus' parable of the wheat and tares:

> The kingdom of heaven is like a man who sowed good
> seed in his field; but while men slept, his enemy came and
> sowed tares among the wheat and went his way. But when
> the grain had sprouted and produced a crop, then the tares
> also appeared. So the servants of the owner came and said to

him, "Sir, did you not sow good seed in your field? How then does it have tares?" He said to them, "An enemy has done this." The servants said to him, "Do you want us then to go and gather them up?" But he said, "No, lest while you gather up the tares you also uproot the wheat with them. Let both grow together until the harvest, and at the time of harvest I will say to the reapers, 'First gather together the tares and bind them in bundles to burn them, but gather the wheat into my barn.'"

—Matthew 13:24–30

In this parable, Jesus compares the kingdom of heaven to a field where a farmer sowed good wheat seeds. However, during the night an enemy sneaked in and sowed *tares* (weeds) among the good crops.

The focus of this parable is on the tares. They represent people who appear righteous and committed but have never been born again. The parable teaches that in the kingdom of heaven these tares will be allowed to coexist with the true believers (symbolized by the wheat) for a period. But at the final judgment, God will separate the wheat from the tares just as a farmer separates the good crop from the weeds during harvest. The tares will be gathered and thrown into the fire, a representation of the ultimate judgment of the wicked.

This parable reminds us to be discerning and not be deceived by appearances alone. It demonstrates that God is the ultimate judge who will reveal the true nature of people's hearts.

The word *tares* used throughout this parable has its roots in the Latin word *zizania*, which is derived from the Greek word *zizanion*.[2] Both words refer to a specific type of weed known as "darnel" (*Lolium temulentum*). Darnel has been called "mimic weed" or "wheat's evil twin" because it looks and grows very much like wheat. But when grown, the weed has a distinctive nature and can produce a variety of debilitating effects. Based on what botanists now know about darnel, I think it's fair to speculate that the tares in Jesus' parable had the following qualities that perhaps symbolize the recent widespread trend of believers falling away from the faith.

Slightly poisonous. Darnel contains toxic alkaloids that, when consumed, can result in symptoms such as nausea, vomiting, and digestive discomfort. On a spiritual level, persistent rejection of God's truth for a "diet" of lies results in a toxic belief system. Most unbelievers reveal their true nature over time; others are genuinely deceived and will face eternity without salvation.

Cause dizziness. Another characteristic of tares is that they can cause dizziness or vertigo when ingested. This concept relates metaphorically to how unbelievers who engage in deceitful or immoral actions might lose their moral compass and experience a sense of spiritual dizziness. They may become disoriented in their beliefs and values, leading to doubts, confusion, a lack of conviction, and finally departure from the faith.

Produce narcotic effects. Tares, due to their toxic properties, can induce narcotic effects when consumed. They can affect a person's vision and speech. Sometimes people would intentionally add darnel to bread or beer to get high.[3] Those who fall away from the church may be influenced by worldly ideologies, temptations, or distractions that gradually numb their spiritual senses.

The point of Jesus' parable was that these potentially destructive tares were going to be allowed to coexist with the good wheat. In the early stages of growth, wheat and darnel are essentially indistinguishable. At that stage, attempting to eliminate the tares would likely damage much good grain.

A Spirit of Fear

At this point we need to make an important distinction. While we continue to follow the botanic metaphor of wheat and weeds, let us also keep in mind that the tares in Jesus' parable represent *people*. If we're only talking about weeds, the destruction they cause in your garden is a chance occurrence. The seeds land there via wind or birds, and the weeds grow, but it's just a random act of nature.

Unlike weeds, people have choices and intentions. Since Jesus taught this parable as an example of the kingdom of heaven, and since the wheat and tares represent people, we need to consider how any of the seed got to be "good." No person starts out as good (Matt. 19:17). Only after we repent, confess our sin, and receive the righteousness that only God can supply do we become "good seed." So the good wheat stalks in Jesus' parable are believers who have placed their trust in Him. In contrast, the tares are people who have rejected God and willfully try to convince others to do the same. The tares were planted there by the enemy for the sole purpose of preventing or inhibiting the growth of the good seed.

The damage people inflict on each other is seldom a random offense. We choose our actions. Even when the harm is unintentional, most of us have an innate sense of right and wrong. When we hurt others, the result should be a feeling of remorse and regret. However, some choose to harden themselves to the feelings of others, as well as to the Word of God and to the Spirit, who convicts them of their ungodly behavior. Yet at some level I believe most of them have an inner, impending spirit of fear of the coming judgment of God. In the parable, the seed that wasn't safely stored in the master's barn was headed for a fiery end.

Believers' encounters with the dark side of the spiritual realm often result in a spirit of fear. My family felt it in Prague. Elisha's servant felt it in Samaria. Perhaps you have felt it in various circumstances. We may think we're doing very well to merely survive in the face of such fears, yet the Bible asserts that our calling as believers extends far beyond that: "God has not given us a spirit of fear, but of power and of love and of a sound mind" (2 Tim. 1:7).

The "spirit of fear" referred to in this verse is not a divine or godly attribute; rather, it represents a state of mind characterized by anxiety, dread, and timidity. It's a condition in which fear dominates one's thoughts and actions, resulting in the person being paralyzed and unable to live in the fullness of faith and love. The spirit of fear can manifest in various ways in our lives, such as fear of the unknown, fear of failure, or fear of rejection. It often hinders personal growth, relationships, and faith.

However, as 2 Timothy 1:7 reminds us, God doesn't just eliminate our fear. He replaces it with a spirit of power, love, and a sound mind. We have the power to overcome this spirit of fear through our faith in God. When we trust in His strength, His love, and His guidance, the Holy Spirit equips us with the strength to overcome our fears, the capacity to love unconditionally, and the clarity of thought to make wise decisions.

It's ironic that if you sense a spirit of fear during overt spiritual warfare, you're probably not the only fearful one. As long as you cling to your faith in Christ, your spiritual opponents are likely to be afraid of you! Scripture tells us, "You believe that there is one God. You do well. Even the demons believe—and tremble!" (Jas. 2:19). And earlier, when we looked at the story of the man possessed by "Legion" (many demons), we saw that Jesus had no problem casting them out. They then pleaded with Him not to destroy them on the spot, negotiating for other options (Mark 5:1–17). (In Luke's account of this story, they "begged Him that he would not command them to go out into the abyss" [Luke 8:31]).

Our spiritual enemies quiver in the presence of Jesus, so our calling is to embody courage and rely on the power of the Holy

Spirit in opposing them. Failure to tap into this divine reservoir not only erodes our emotional and mental health but also risks yielding ground to the enemy.

REKINDLE COURAGE

Every fear we encounter in life is commensurate with our potential to overcome it. If a fear seems overwhelming, it is crucial to remember it is matched with your inherent capability to confront it in the power of God. As you devote yourself to overcoming it, your potential and ability to handle bigger fears will expand. The ultimate resolution of all our fears is found in trusting God.

Our future is unpredictable, filled with moments of joy, sorrow, or neutrality. By tackling each day with faith, relying on God's divine strength, and recognizing that He is revealing the future one step at a time, we learn to manage our fears effectively. This step-by-step approach fosters a cycle of continuous growth and spiritual enrichment, allowing us to decipher life's complexities and better understand God's divine plans. It fortifies our faith, making us resilient against life's uncertainties, reinforcing our spiritual resolve against the daily battles and fears we encounter.

Every generation is presented with a unique set of fears, intended as both challenges and opportunities for spiritual growth, learning, and divine blessings. By acknowledging this, we can transform our perspective on fears, seeing them as gateways to higher spiritual wisdom and deeper insights in God's Word.

To contemplate God is to realize that He navigates us through life's maze one step at a time, allowing us to experience, learn, and grow in harmony with His divine wisdom and timing. This realization fills our souls with divine insight, empowering us to journey through life with grace, resilience, and unwavering faith in His eternal love and guidance.

Two Antidotes to Fear

Thanksgiving and praise are fundamental aspects of our faith journey, and they play a significant role in our relationship with God. These two actions are immediate responses to God's promises and provisions, demonstrating our trust and faith in Him. When we receive a promise from God, we can cast away fear and embrace the promise. And rather than waiting for the *fulfillment* of the promise, we should learn to express our gratitude and praise to God as soon as we receive it, as an act of faith.

An illustration of this principle can be found during the reign of King Jehoshaphat in Judah (2 Chron. 20). Jehoshaphat was one of the few godly kings of Israel and Judah after the kingdom was divided. He received a distressing report that a coalition of enemy nations had assembled a vast and formidable army that was advancing toward Judah. Recognizing the insurmountable odds he faced, he turned to God in humility and gathered his people for united prayer and fasting.

In response to their heartfelt plea for help, God spoke through a Levite, delivering a prophetic message to Jehoshaphat. The message was clear: "Do not be afraid nor dismayed because of this great multitude, for the battle is not yours, but God's.... You will not need to fight in this battle. Position yourselves, stand still and see the salvation of the LORD, who is with you" (2 Chron. 20:15, 17).

Remarkably, Jehoshaphat didn't hesitate to trust in God's promise, even though the enemy army still loomed on the horizon. He exercised faith in God's word with an impromptu praise and worship service. Then the very next day he led his people to confront the enemy. Jehoshaphat's conviction that God would be true to His word was evidenced by his unorthodox battle strategy:

> So they rose early in the morning and…as they went out, Jehoshaphat stood and said, "Hear me, O Judah and you inhabitants of Jerusalem: Believe in the LORD your God, and you shall be established; believe His prophets, and you shall prosper." And when he had consulted with the people, he appointed those who should sing to the LORD, and who should praise the beauty of holiness, as they went out before the army and were saying: "Praise the LORD, for His mercy endures forever."
>
> —2 CHRONICLES 20:20–21

This act of praise was an extraordinary display of faith. What kind of king sends his *singers* out to battle first, instead of positioning his strongest soldiers at the front lines? By placing the worship and praise leaders there, Jehoshaphat demonstrated that he believed God's word and trusted in His promise of deliverance.

What followed was nothing short of miraculous. As Jehoshaphat's army approached the battlefield, confusion spread among the enemy ranks, leading them to turn on one another. By the time Jehoshaphat's forces arrived, the combined tribes had already killed one another off. No one had escaped. It took the forces of Judah three days to collect all the spoil. And after that, the fear of God in the surrounding kingdoms ensured that no one messed with Jehoshaphat again (2 Chron. 20:24–30).

This historical account vividly illustrates the power of immediate thanksgiving and praise in response to God's promises. Jehoshaphat's faith and obedience in accepting God's word and expressing gratitude even before the battle was fought became the catalyst for a supernatural intervention and a resounding victory.

In our own lives, we can learn from Jehoshaphat's example. When we receive God's promises, whether in His Word or through personal revelation, let us respond with unwavering faith, immediate thanksgiving, and heartfelt praise. Just as God honored Jehoshaphat's faith, He will honor ours, guiding us through the battles we face and ultimately leading us to victory. Thanksgiving and praise are not merely acts of gratitude; they are expressions of faith and trust in the unfailing promises of our heavenly Father.

This account of King Jehoshaphat underscores two vital principles that are applicable to our faith journey and relationship with God.

First, it teaches us that God expects us to praise Him for the promises He gives us, without waiting to see them fulfilled. Jehoshaphat received a divine promise from God (through a prophetic utterance) that God would deliver him and his people from the impending threat of a vast enemy army. The crucial key is that Jehoshaphat didn't delay his response. He didn't wait until the victory was achieved or the enemy was defeated to start praising God. The fact that God had made the promise was reason enough to respond immediately in praise and worship. When has God never kept a promise?

This principle challenges us to embrace the promises of God with unwavering faith and gratitude. It encourages us to trust that God's Word is true and reliable, and His promises will come to pass in His perfect timing. We shouldn't withhold our praise until we see the fulfillment of those promises. Instead, our praise should flow as an expression of faith and trust in God's character and His faithfulness to His Word.

Second, the story teaches us that praise offered in faith releases the supernatural intervention of God on our behalf. When Jehoshaphat and his people praised God with confidence in His promise, it set in motion a series of supernatural events. The enemy forces were thrown into confusion, and they ended up defeating themselves. God intervened in a remarkable way, and Jehoshaphat and his people witnessed a miraculous victory.

This principle highlights the profound impact of faith-filled praise. What kind of faith does it take to praise God only *after* you get what you're asking for? Our praise should never be just a passive response to God's goodness; it should be an active, faith-driven catalyst for God's intervention in our lives. When we praise God amid challenges, it not only strengthens our faith but also invites God's supernatural power to work on our behalf. It's a reminder that our battles are ultimately His battles because He is our source of strength and deliverance.

In summary, the account of Jehoshaphat teaches us that faith begins to praise God before the promised victory, not merely after it. It urges us to trust God's promises, praise Him for them without delay, and understand that our praise is a powerful tool that invites His supernatural intervention. This timeless lesson encourages us to live a life of faith that is marked by immediate, unwavering praise in response to God's promises, knowing that He is faithful to fulfill them in His perfect way and timing.

Chapter 14

Wisdom and Faith

ANYONE WHO COMES to California to shop for real estate quickly learns that those looking for "affordable housing" need not bother. Newcomers who see the price tags on houses and buildings around here are likely to register enough sticker shock to charge a defibrillator. And unfortunately pastors are not immune to the fears and stresses of financing a sprawling, growing church.

When we selected the location for Influence Church, we placed a lot of money in escrow and went looking for a loan. No problem, right? Well, as time wound down toward our closing date, we had been turned down by something like 113 banks. We got down to the Monday before the scheduled closing the following Monday—five business days away. I was a nervous wreck because I still couldn't find a nickel in a couch. It didn't help when everyone kept asking me, "What are you going to do?" My unspoken answer to them was always, "If I knew what I was going to do, I would have already done it!" But in my role as a faithful and confident pastor, my outward response was, "We're just going to believe God wants us to have this building and trust Him to provide for us."

Someone gave me a contact in Amarillo, Texas, so I contacted the guy. He told me, "No, I can't help you, but you can try calling this other guy." I'm thinking, "Lord, have mercy. Now we're up to 114 nos, and we're in danger of losing our money in escrow." This experience wasn't helping my self-esteem.

Still, I called the other guy and told him how much money we needed. He said, "Yes, I think we can do that." I told him we had to close on Monday, and he said that wouldn't be a problem. I asked if he would expedite the application, and he said, "Sure." But after I waited all afternoon and didn't receive anything, I called him back. He told me, "Well, I had a long lunch. I'll get it to you tomorrow."

On Tuesday the application arrived, and I completed it in record time. After all, I'd filled out 113 of them. I was careful to avoid anything that might create a delay. *Collateral? Sure. Here's my house, car, firstborn child. Take them. We need to get this building.* Unbeknownst to him, we were also needing and praying for an additional $200,000 that wasn't covered in the loan. We were going to try to raise it on our own, but I wasn't about to mention it to him and jeopardize this opportunity. I sent the application back to him and followed up in a couple of hours. "Hey, did you get it?"

"No. Not yet. I took off early this afternoon." I was speechless, which is a good thing, or I might have said something not very pastor-like. So now it's Wednesday. He calls me and says, "I have good news. You've got approval from the Junior Loan Committee." The word that stuck in my ear was *junior*. I asked, "Is there a Senior Loan Committee?"

"Oh, yes."

"When do *they* meet?"

"Tomorrow."

That would be Thursday. I was running out of days here. But

sure enough, he called me on Thursday and said, "I've got some good news and some bad news. Which do you want?"

I said, "Give me the bad news first."

"It turns out that we can't close on your loan on Monday…"

Well, yeah, that's pretty bad news.

"…so we're going to close tomorrow." And before I could hardly register what he was saying, he added, "But as we were looking at the loan, we don't think you asked for enough money. We'd like to add another $200,000, if that's OK." I had made no mention of what we were praying for. We signed the papers on Friday. As we did, I was physically exhausted but spiritually exhilarated.

What did I learn from this trying experience? Let me just say that a few years after securing this loan for our church, we needed to add a ministry center. We prayed about it, committed to a $6 million building, and again had trouble finding a loan. But that time it didn't really bother me because I'd been down that road. I'd learned from experience that if your faith is in God rather than your processes, everything will be fine because you don't have to know how and when your prayers will be answered. God may just surprise you. Every time you go down a faith journey, your faith increases.

Maybe you've had a similar experience of how God occasionally sends an unsettling situation or person (like my lackadaisical loan officer) into your life to increase your faith, almost against your will. It's not like anyone ever prays, "God, I want You to take as long as You possibly can to answer my prayer." Yet God often has good reason for delaying before He responds. Abraham had to wait twenty-five years to receive the heir God had promised him, but during that time he learned much about God and the importance of faith, obedience, and patience. And when we see that God indeed acts eventually, our faith is strengthened.

A Long History of Problems

If you study the great movements of God, spiritual revivals always come at a low moment in history. They don't come at the height of prosperity when everyone's comfortable but when people are feeling a desperation for God. We dream, plan, ponder, and set goals, often while neglecting to include God in our plans. We tend to forget that we can't accomplish anything in our own wisdom and strength, so God sometimes allows and arranges situations to bring us closer to Him.

Think about American history. Every generation has had new problems to solve. We started as colonists under British rule. The next generations had to fight for freedom and then create a new system of government. As others immigrated into this new land of liberty, the problem became exploration and expansion. Along the way, we made some mistakes, including the establishment of slavery and too-frequent mistreatment of indigenous peoples. Freeing the slaves brought a new problem—the Civil War. A few generations later came the Great War, World War I, supposedly "the war to end all wars." Following that came a time of prosperity, but then we went through the Great Depression. Then World War II. Then Korea. Then the Vietnam War, which created new problems at home with much social unrest and many protests. The civil rights movement added to the turmoil.

As we look back through our history, we see the results of our forefathers' toughness, tenacity, courage, and perseverance. We take great pride in our history and what we have achieved as a country, yet as we reflect on this long string of difficulties and problem-solving, many of us neglect to acknowledge that along the way God also provided powerful manifestations of His Spirit.

America experienced a Great Awakening—an extended spiritual revival—during the first half of the 1700s as God inspired powerful preachers to emphasize the importance of faith, grace, repentance, and Scripture. People responded in large numbers, and some of those people became our Founding Fathers. A Second Great Awakening occurred in the 1790s and resulted in the formation of many colleges, seminaries, and missions organizations. Some believe a Third Great Awakening ran from the late 1850s into the twentieth century.[1]

As we look back and praise the human efforts of those who came before us, we need to remember that *they* tended to give the credit to God. When determining our national motto, they didn't decide on "In courage and tenacity we trust," or "In our own strength we trust." They acknowledged God's divine protection and provision throughout the formation and maintenance of our nation, and they realized God is the only consistently reliable source in whom we can trust. (We saw several examples in chapter 2, "An Appeal to Heaven.")

Today's church needs to learn this same lesson. Our problems often disguise themselves. We think we have financial problems, or physical problems, or relationship problems. But what is behind all those issues is a *wisdom* problem. Every problem you face is ultimately a wisdom problem. And believe it or not, that's good news!

The great thing about wisdom is that if you lack it, you only need to ask for it. However, there's a right way and a wrong way to ask: "If any of you lacks wisdom, let him ask of God, who gives to all liberally and without reproach, and it will be given to him. But let him ask in faith, with no doubting, for he who doubts is like a wave of the sea driven and tossed by the wind. For let not that man suppose that he will receive anything from the Lord; he is a double-minded man, unstable in all his ways" (Jas. 1:5–8).

Lots of people can offer us the wisdom of age and experience, but the wisdom from God is on a whole different level. It is wisdom from above that provides insights into a situation you could never realize on your own. God offers this wisdom "liberally and without reproach," yet a fertile mind and a spiritual hunger and thirst are required to comprehend it.

Believers are called to engage this world with supernatural ability and manifest God's kingdom, but it takes wisdom from God to do so. We're often quick to impose our political views on the people in our circles of influence, or our trivial opinions about music, sports teams, and every little thing. But when we're among others, we should be offering them the wisdom of God.

Some of us are willing to talk to others about anything and everything *except* God because we think we might offend them or open ourselves up to ridicule. We don't want people to get the wrong impression about us. When I was younger, I worried all the time about what other people thought about me. But one day my dad gave me a good piece of wisdom. He told me that while I was so worried about how others saw me, they weren't even thinking about me at all. It made sense. I had better things to do than sit around thinking about them, so why would they think about me?

A Lesson From Zerubbabel

Our Founding Fathers had good biblical precedent for putting their trust in God, and so do we. The Book of Zechariah is a seldom-read portion of Scripture for many people, yet it is packed with powerful insights. In one portion, God delivered an assuring message for the prophet Zechariah to give to an Israelite leader, Zerubbabel, who was facing hard challenges.

Zerubbabel was from one of the Israelite families exiled to Babylon after Nebuchadnezzar destroyed Jerusalem and the temple, and he was among the first to return after being given permission to do so. He had been designated "governor of Judah" (Hag. 1:1) and was put in charge of organizing workers to rebuild the altar and the temple (Ezra 3:2, 8). His crew had completed the foundation of the temple, but then he ran into opposition from a lot of local adversaries trying their best to prevent the rebuilding project. They were appealing to the Persian leadership, and while waiting for a response they had suspended work on the temple and dampened the spirits of the people.

God sent Zechariah to Zerubbabel with this message:

> This is the word of the LORD to Zerubbabel: "Not by might nor by power, but by My Spirit," says the LORD of hosts. "Who are you, O great mountain? Before Zerubbabel you shall become a plain! And he shall bring forth the capstone with shouts of 'Grace, grace to it!'" Moreover the word of the LORD came to me, saying: "The hands of Zerubbabel have laid the foundation of this temple; his hands shall also finish it."
> —ZECHARIAH 4:6–9

It didn't take long for God's promise to be fulfilled. Shortly thereafter, an official decree went out from Persian king Darius to authorize the temple rebuilding. Darius even volunteered to pay for the entire project and to return the sacred items that Nebuchadnezzar had taken from the original temple. And to prevent further delay, Darius imposed a restraining order to keep Zerubbabel's opponents away from the worksite (Ezra 6:1–12).

Work resumed and the temple was completed while Zechariah and another prophet, Haggai, were there to preach and encourage the builders (vv. 14–15). After the temple was restored, the returned exiles had Passover together and a weeklong celebration of joy (vv. 19–22). Now *that's* a revival.

God's reminder to Zechariah is just as applicable to us: we won't resolve our problems in our own might and power but through His Spirit. Do you suppose our Founding Fathers acknowledged this truth as they were laying the groundwork for what would eventually become the greatest nation on the planet? I like to think so. But an even more important question is, Do *you* acknowledge this truth as you face today's problems as an individual, a member of your community, and a citizen of your nation? When faced with a particularly threatening problem, do you instinctively flail at the problem in your own strength, using every resource at your disposal? Or is your first response to rely on the Spirit of God to provide the strength, wisdom, and persistence to overcome the problem?

Pastor Lester Sumrall said that God will never give you a dream you can accomplish on your own. I agree, yet reliance on the Spirit of God isn't mutually exclusive with doing what we can to improve the situation. We're not to sit by idly and wait for God to remove all the obstacles in our lives. When we're confronted with problems, I don't think God is pleased if all we do is moan and complain to Him about it. I know people who could be professional moaners, but complaints don't resolve problems. Jesus challenges His followers to act with His authority and on His behalf. But the starting point is to secure the wisdom and direction of the Spirit of God.

This was never clearer than in the case of the father who brought his demon-possessed son to Jesus' disciples to be healed. Three of the disciples were away with Jesus on a nearby mountain to witness Jesus being transfigured. They saw His face shine like the sun and His clothes become dazzlingly white as He spoke with Moses and Elijah (Matt. 17:1–3). But afterward, when Jesus and the three descended, they found a crowd. The father of the boy ran to Jesus and begged Him to heal his son because His disciples had been unable to.

This father was persistent and determined. If your son or daughter were suffering, wouldn't you do anything to provide help and healing? So when the disciples' power proved insufficient, the troubled dad went straight to Jesus, who rebuked the demon and healed the boy immediately.

The disciples had previously been able to cast out demons (Mark 6:13), so they privately asked Jesus what had gone wrong. Jesus had already given them a clue. Just prior to healing the boy, He said to the crowd, "O faithless and perverse generation, how long shall I be with you? How long shall I bear with you"? (Matt. 17:17). So here, in private, Jesus was more specific. When they asked, "Why could we not cast it out?" He told them, "Because of your unbelief; for assuredly, I say to you, if you have faith as a mustard seed, you will say to this mountain, 'Move from here to there,' and it will move; and nothing will be impossible for you. However, this kind does not go out except by prayer and fasting" (Matt. 17:19–21).

Jesus highlighted the problem as the faithlessness of the whole generation and the unbelief of the disciples, specifically. They'd had a spiritual problem to deal with, and they tried to handle it casually, without proper preparation. If they weren't seeing the power of God they had been given, they needed to acknowledge their authority and position and they would see the miracles of God take place.

As we look at Zechariah's message to Zerubbabel and Jesus' message to His spiritually ineffective disciples, we see a common theme. Jesus says that faith "as a mustard seed" can move mountains. Zechariah also referred to mountain moving as he spoke about God's Spirit accomplishing feats that human might and power cannot. That mountain-sized problem Zerubbabel was facing? "You shall become a plain!" The temple was completed and the capstone put into place as the people shouted praises to God. That mountain-sized problem the disciples couldn't budge? It was demolished by Jesus, empowered by the Spirit of God. The young boy was immediately healed from his long period of spiritual oppression. Yes, faith does indeed move mountains.

Zechariah had more to say about moving mountains as God showed him visions of the future. It's interesting that just prior to his "Not by might nor by power" statement, he had a vision of a gold lampstand and two olive trees (Zech. 4:2–3)—all connected to events of the end times (Rev. 1:12–13; 11:3–4). Later he envisioned the Lord standing atop the Mount of Olives, which "shall be split in two, from east to west, making a very large valley" (Zech. 14:4). I think Zechariah wanted us to know that during times of tribulation, we're going to have power, we're going to have a witness, we're going to have authority—not on our own but because of the Spirit of the Lord in our lives.

LEVELS OF FAITH

Faith is enduring like a mustard seed. Seeds have been recovered from the pyramids that were well over two thousand years old, and they still grew when planted. Time doesn't diminish the effectiveness of faith. Distance doesn't affect the power of faith. For many people, "Seeing is believing," but we in God's church need to remember that "we walk by faith, not by sight" (2 Cor. 5:7).

If you study faith and Scripture, you will find at least five different kinds of descriptors for faith. As you read through these, consider where you might be on this scale.

Weak faith

When you fail to exercise, your muscles begin to atrophy and your entire body becomes weak. The same is true on a spiritual level. Some people become believers but never exercise their faith. They mechanically practice Christian rites and rituals without ever strengthening their personal relationship with Christ. They remain satisfied with a bottle-fed "milk" diet and never get into the "meat" of the gospel (1 Cor. 3:2; Heb. 5:13). The apostle Paul says to "receive" such people and respect where they are in their spiritual journey (Rom. 14:1–13). Yet at this stage their weak faith causes them to miss much of the Christian freedom that is available to them.

Little faith

The storms of life often expose the insufficiency of our faith. It was a literal storm that got the disciples' attention one day on the Sea of Galilee. Although several of them were experienced fishermen, the suddenness and magnitude of this storm had them all fearful of drowning. Jesus was fatigued and sleeping, but the disciples' panic finally drove them to wake Him up. Before doing anything else, Jesus asked them, "Why are you fearful, O you of little faith?" (Matt. 8:26). Jesus was in the boat with them. He had already told them they were going to cross to the other side. Didn't they believe Him? People with little faith can have Jesus right there with them and still believe they are "perishing" (Luke 8:22–24).

Growing faith

People with growing faith have a different response to the difficulties of life. Paul commended the church in Thessalonica for their growing faith: "We are bound to thank God always for you, brethren, as it is fitting, because your faith grows exceedingly, and the love of every one of you all abounds toward each other, so that we ourselves boast of you among the churches of God for your patience and faith in all your persecutions and tribulations that you endure" (2 Thess. 1:3–4).

Excitement builds when your faith grows and you really begin to believe that you can trust God to see you through whatever happens in life.

Strong faith

Using Abraham as an example, Paul describes the significance of strong faith. God had promised Abraham many descendants, yet he didn't even have an heir, and he was getting up in years. But meanwhile Abraham was developing a strong faith in God. Paul writes: "Not being weak in faith, he did not consider his own body, already dead (since he was about a hundred years old), and the deadness of Sarah's womb. He did not waver at the promise of God through unbelief, but was strengthened in faith, giving glory to God, and being fully convinced that what He had promised He was also able to perform. And therefore 'it was accounted to him for righteousness'" (Rom. 4:19–22).

And perhaps Abraham's faith was never stronger than after God gave him that heir, Isaac, and then asked him to sacrifice the young boy to Him. Many people read this account and wonder how any parent could respond to such a request, but an explanation is given in Hebrews:

> By faith Abraham, when he was tested, offered up Isaac, and he who had received the promises offered up his only begotten son, of whom it was said, "In Isaac your seed shall be called," concluding that God was able to raise him up, even from the dead."
>
> —Hebrews 11:17–19

God didn't allow Abraham to go through with the sacrifice, of course (Gen. 21:1–18). In response to Abraham's unparalleled faith, God confirmed the covenant He had made with the patriarch. But don't miss the significance of *why* Abraham was willing to comply with God's request. Although no one had ever been resurrected from the dead at that time, and the very thought was unlikely to have crossed anyone's mind, Abraham believed it had to be possible for Isaac to live again because that was the only way God could fulfill the covenant He had made. Strong faith sustains hope in seemingly hopeless situations and provides strength even in our weakest moments.

Great faith

Rarely do you find someone with *great* faith. Abraham's obedience to God concerning Isaac should probably go in this category. But Jesus cited an example during His earthly ministry, and it wasn't someone you would ever expect. A Roman centurion approached Jesus one day and pleaded with Him to heal one of his servants who was paralyzed. Jesus agreed to go with the soldier, yet the centurion told Him not to bother: "Lord, I am not worthy that You should come under my roof. But only speak a word, and my servant will be healed. For I also am a man under authority, having soldiers under me. And I say to this one, 'Go,' and he goes; and to another 'Come,' and he comes; and to my servant, 'Do this,' and he does it."

Jesus "marveled" at the centurion's response and told the surrounding crowd, "Assuredly, I say to you, I have not found such great faith, not even in Israel!" (Matt. 8:5–10) And He healed the servant that hour.

This Roman soldier somehow comprehended Jesus' power and spiritual authority at a level that not even Jesus' own disciples were able to fathom.

A BONUS BENEFIT

"Not by might nor by power, but by [God's] Spirit." We've seen how the power of God abounds in our lives when we yield to His Spirit rather than relying solely on our own strength and skills. And yielding to God's Spirit has another beneficial result: *freedom*. Paul writes, "Now the Lord is the Spirit; and where the Spirit of the Lord is, there is liberty" (2 Cor. 3:17). And elsewhere he adds: "Stand fast therefore in the liberty by which Christ has made us free, and do not be entangled again with a yoke of bondage" (Gal. 5:1).

Christian freedom is not what a lot of people think it is. It isn't the ability to do whatever you want to do. Real freedom is the ability to choose properly under the auspices of God's kingdom. As you respond to God's Spirit in faith, you discover you're working and living out your life the way God wants you to. You're determined to break free of all the worldly entanglements that keep you from becoming the person God created you to be.

Faith can be challenging at times and is often misunderstood: "Now faith is the substance of things hoped for, the evidence of things not seen" (Heb. 11:1). Since we can't *see* faith, a lot of people equate it with positive thinking: "I just choose to believe that everything's going to work out OK." And then when everything doesn't work out as they expected, they have a crisis of faith. Some even reject God and experience a "shipwreck" of their faith (1 Tim. 1:19).

Genuine faith always has an object; it is faith *in God*. "By faith we understand that the worlds were framed by the word of God" (Heb. 11:3). If you know God's Word, if you know God has promised something, you can have faith that it is true because "the grass withers, the flower fades, but the word of our God stands forever" (Isa. 40:8). Do you know what that means? It means the Word of God will be in heaven with you, so you might as well get familiar with it now!

The themes of wisdom and faith are spread throughout the Scriptures with different emphases and applications. Never have they been needed more than now. They are the qualities that will see us through the darkest of times. They enable us to discern between God's truth and the very convincing lies that will deceive many as the last days approach. Wisdom and faith keep us plugged into God's power and His Spirit when no other options seem to work. And they are the foundation for Christian liberty. Once you experience the glorious freedom that only Christ can provide, you are "free indeed" (John 8:36).

I hope this book has helped to increase your awareness of how today's events appear to be aligning with biblical prophecy. Even more, I hope your confidence has been renewed that everything is going to plan according to God's timetable. No matter what happens, His sovereignty is unshakable.

It's almost midnight in America, but after midnight comes the dawning of the Day of the Lord. In preparation for that day, it is my prayer that in the weeks and months and years to come you will become wiser, be more faithful, and experience more of the freedom that only God can provide.

Notes

Chapter 1

1. George Orwell, *1984* (New York: Signet Classic, 1961).
2. Albert Biderman, "Biderman's Chart of Coercion," University of Strathclyde, accessed October 5, 2023, https://www.strath.ac.uk/media/1newwebsite/departmentsubject/socialwork/documents/eshe/Bidermanschartofcoercion.pdf.
3. The link to the full exchange can be found at https://www.insidernj.com/murphy-tangles-tucker-constitutional-lockdown-questions-wasnt-thinking-bill-rights/.
4. See the Book of Daniel, chapters 3 and 6.

Chapter 2

1. Kevin Dutton and John Collins, "How to Complete an Impossible Challenge," *Psyche*, August 3, 2022, https://psyche.co/guides/how-to-complete-an-impossible-challenge-using-the-god-principle.
2. William Wirt, *Sketches of the Life and Character of Patrick Henry* (Philadelphia, 1836) as reproduced in *The World's Great Speeches*, Lewis Copeland and Lawrence W. Lamm, eds., (New York, 1973), Colonial Williamsburg, March 3, 2020, colonialwilliamsburg.org/learn/deep-dives/give-me-liberty-or-give-me-death/.
3. John Locke, "Right of Revolution," Second Treatise, 1689, https://press-pubs.uchicago.edu/founders/documents/v1ch3s2.html#:~:text=For%20all%20Power%20given%20with,for%20their%20safety%20and%20security.
4. John Locke, "Right of Revolution."
5. John Locke, "Right of Revolution."
6. John Locke, "Right of Revolution."
7. "The 'Famous Five,'" United States Senate, accessed October 6, 2023, https://www.senate.gov/artandhistory/history/common/briefing/Famous_Five_Seven.htm.
8. From a speech given June 3, 1834, as quoted by John Bartlett, *Bartlett's Familiar Quotations* (Boston: Little, Brown, 1855, 1980), 451.

9.   Daniel Webster, "The First Bunker Hill Monument Oration," June 17, 1825, https://www.bartleby.com/lit-hub/hc/america-ii-1818-1865/i-the-first-bunker-hill-monument-oration/.

10. "An Address Delivered Before the New York Historical Society, February 23, 1852," Scholars Junction, https://scholarsjunction.msstate.edu/cgi/viewcontent.cgi?article=1691&context=fvw-pamphlets.

11. Richard Booker, *The Lamb and the Seven-Sealed Scroll* (Shippensburg, PA: Destiny Image, 2012).

12. Paul E. Billheimer, *Destined for the Throne* (Ft. Washington, PA: Christian Literature Crusade, 1975), 60.

13. Andy Andrews, *The Traveler's Gift* (Nashville: Thomas Nelson, 2005).

14. Quoted by B. D. Hobbs, "Get Ready: Big Tech to Unveil Communist Style Social Credit System on U.S.," Houston's News Radio 740 KTRH, January 14, 2021, https://ktrh.iheart.com/content/2021-01-13-get-ready-big-tech-to-unveil-communist-style-social-credit-system-on-us/.

15. "PBS Lawyer Resigns After Being Caught in Veritas Sting," AP News, January 12, 2021, https://apnews.com/article/donald-trump-entertainment-coronavirus-pandemic-8f586d687ab332777a7a059457ff818e.

CHAPTER 3

1.   "A Time of Unprecedented Danger: It Is 90 Seconds to Midnight," *Bulletin of the Atomic Scientists*, January 24, 2023, https://thebulletin.org/doomsday-clock/.

2.   "This Week in Jewish History: Israel Victorious in Six-Day War," World Jewish Congress, June 5, 2023, https://www.worldjewishcongress.org/en/news/this-week-in-jewish-history—israel-victorious-in-six-day-war-6-2-2020.

3.   For more information, see https://www.jewishvirtuallibrary.org/jerusalem-islamic-waqf.

4.   William T. Reynolds, "Horror in Harbor on 9/11," *Times Union*, September 5, 2021, https://www.timesunion.com/opinion/article/Horror-in-harbor-on-9-11-16435916.php.

CHAPTER 4

1. C. S. Lewis, *Mere Christianity* (San Francisco: HarperSanFrancisco, 1952), 52.

2. See my previous book, *One Nation Without Law* (Ada, MI: Chosen Books, 2017).

3. Julia Ainsley, "The Biden Administration Is Turning a Lower Percentage of Border-crossing Migrants Back into Mexico," NBC News, August 23, 2023, https://www.nbcnews.com/politics/immigration/biden-lower-percentage-border-crossing-migrants-mexico-rcna100966.

4. Tatiana Almeida, "The Most Urgent Refugee Crises Around the World," World Vision, updated June 8, 2023, by Alicia Dubay.

5. Miriam Berger, "A Guide to How Gender-Neutral Language Is Developing Around the World," *Washington Post*, December 15, 2019, https://www.washingtonpost.com/world/2019/12/15/guide-how-gender-neutral-language-is-developing-around-world/.

6. Charlie Warzel and Stuart A. Thompson, "They Stormed the Capitol. Their Apps Tracked Them," *New York Times*, February 5, 2021, https://www.nytimes.com/2021/02/05/opinion/capitol-attack-cellphone-data.html.

7. Warzel and Thompson, "They Stormed the Capitol."

8. Klaus Schwab, "A Better Economy Is Possible. But We Need to Reimagine Capitalism to Do It," *Time*, October 21, 2020, https://time.com/collection/great-reset/5900748/klaus-schwab-capitalism/.

9. Klaus Schwab, "Now Is the Time for a 'Great Reset,'" World Economic Forum, June 3, 2020, https://www.weforum.org/agenda/2020/06/now-is-the-time-for-a-great-reset.

10. Katie Canales and Aaron Mok, "China's 'Social Credit' System Ranks Citizens and Punishes Them With Throttled Internet Speeds and Flight Bans if the Communist Party Deems Them Untrustworthy," *Business Insider*, November 28, 2022, https://www.businessinsider.com/china-social-credit-system-punishments-and-rewards-explained-2018-4.

11. Canales and Mok, "China's 'Social Credit' System Ranks Citizens..."

12. Rachel Botsman, "Big Data Meets Big Brother as China Moves to Rate Its Citizens," *Wired*, October, 21, 2017, https://www.wired.co.uk/article/chinese-government-social-credit-score-privacy-invasion.

Chapter 5

1. "Frank Wisner," Spartacus Educational, accessed October 30, 2023, https://spartacus-educational.com/JFKwisner.htm.
2. "Operation Mockingbird," Spartacus Educational, accessed October 30, 2023, https://spartacus-educational.com/JFKmockingbird.htm.
3. Martin Young, "IMF Touts Programmable and Controllable CBDC for 'Financial Inclusion,'" Be(In)Crypto, October 17, 2022, https://beincrypto.com/imf-touts-programmable-controllable-cbdc-financial-inclusion.

Chapter 6

1. Michael Kennedy, "Horror Movies Make More Profit—Here's Why," Screen Rant, January 1, 2020, https://screenrant.com/horror-movies-more-profit-reason.
2. C. S. Lewis, *The Screwtape Letters* (New York: HarperOne, 1942, 1996), ix.
3. Lewis, *The Screwtape Letters*, 16.
4. Lewis, *The Screwtape Letters*, 60–61.
5. "Roman Legions: The Backbone of the Roman Military," History Extra, accessed October 31, 2023, https://www.historyextra.com/period/roman/roman-legion-how-fight-how-many-men-weapons-armour-legionary-centurion.

Chapter 7

1. Campbell Robertson, "Iraq Suffers as the Euphrates River Dwindles," *New York Times*, July 13, 2009, https://www.nytimes.com/2009/07/14/world/middleeast/14euphrates.html.
2. "Red China: Firecracker No. 2," *Time*, May 21, 1965, https://content.time.com/time/subscriber/article/0,33009,901693,00.html.
3. "Were China's Genetically-Modified 'Super Soldiers' Predicted in Bible Prophecy?," Back to Jerusalem, accessed November 2, 2023, https://backtojerusalem.com/were-chinas-genetically-modified-super-soldiers-predicted-in-bible-prophecy.
4. Elsa B. Kania and Wilson VornDick, "China's Military Biotech Frontier: CRISPR, Military-Civil Fusion, and the New Revolution in Military Affairs," The Jamestown Foundation, October 8, 2019, https://jamestown.org/program/chinas-military-biotech-frontier-crispr-military-civil-fusion-and-the-new-revolution-in-military-affairs.

5. Sui-Lee Wee, "China Is Collecting DNA From Tens of Millions of Men and Boys, Using U.S. Equipment," *New York Times*, June 17, 2020, https://www.nytimes.com/2020/06/17/world/asia/China-DNA-surveillance.html.

6. Jon Wertheim, "China's Push to Control Americans' Health Care Future," CBS News, January 31, 2021, https://www.cbsnews.com/news/biodata-dna-china-collection-60-minutes-2021-01-31.

7. Wertheim, "China's Push to Control Americans' Health Care Future."

8. Greg Myre, "China Wants Your Data—and May Already Have It," NPR, February 24, 2021, https://www.npr.org/2021/02/24/969532277/china-wants-your-data-and-may-already-have-it.

9. Julian E. Barnes, "U.S. Warns of Efforts by China to Collect Genetic Data," *New York Times*, October 22, 2021, https://www.nytimes.com/2021/10/22/us/politics/china-genetic-data-collection.html.

10. Adam Chan, "CFIUS, Team Telecom, and China," Lawfare, September 28, 2021, https://www.lawfaremedia.org/article/cfius-team-telecom-and-china.

11. ListGlobally Marketing, May, 2019, https://blog.listglobally.com/en/25-of-foreign-investment-in-u-s-residential-real-estate-was-made-by-chinese.

12. Emily Washburn, "How Much U.S. Farmland Does China Really Own?" *Forbes*, March 1, 2023, https://www.forbes.com/sites/emilywashburn/2023/03/01/how-much-us-farmland-does-china-really-own-more-than-bill-gates-and-less-than-17-other-countries/?sh=169c0444421f.

13. Andrew Hall, "Voices of the Persecuted Church (Part 1): The Chinese Underground Church," The Washington Stand, December 29, 2022, https://washingtonstand.com/commentary/voices-of-the-persecuted-church-part-1-the-chinese-underground-church.

14. Marian L. Tupy, "100 Years of Communism: Death and Deprivation," CATO Institute, October 28, 2017, https://www.cato.org/commentary/100-years-communism-death-deprivation.

15. John F. Walvoord, "Chapter XII The Kings of the East: The Oriental Confederacy," *The Nations in Prophecy*, accessed November 3, 2023, https://walvoord.com/article/303.

16. "Amity Celebrates Its 200 Millionth Printed Bible," Nanjing Amity Printing Co., Ltd., November 23, 2019, http://www.amityprinting.com/en/gsyw/info.aspx?itemid=245.

17. Nina Shea, "China's Threat to the Bible," VirtueOnline, December 23, 2020, https://virtueonline.org/chinas-threat-bible.

18. Shea, "China's Threat to the Bible."

19. Shea, "China's Threat to the Bible."

20. "The Greater Miracle: Amity Press Prints Its 200 Millionth Bible," United Bible Societies, September 16, 2020, https://ubscp.org/the-greater-miracle-200-millionth-bible.

21. Dr. Ewelina U. Ochab, "Let China Sleep, for When She Wakes, She Will Shake the World," *Forbes*, January 13, 2021, https://www.forbes.com/sites/ewelinaochab/2021/01/13/let-china-sleep-for-when-she-wakes-she-will-shake-the-world/?sh=6b5665256537.

Chapter 8

1. Jeffrey M. Jones, "Belief in God in U.S. Dips to 81%, a New Low," Gallup, June 17, 2022, https://news.gallup.com/poll/393737/belief-god-dips-new-low.aspx.

Chapter 9

1. Rabbi Daniel Lapin, "Only Six More Years?," July 14, 2020, https://rabbidaniellapin.com/only-six-more-years.

2. Adam Drakos, "Tytler's Cycle of Civilizations," ThinkingWest, November 16, 2022, https://thinkingwest.com/2022/11/16/tytlers-cycle-of-civilizations.

3. Henry Wadsworth Longfellow, "The Village Blacksmith," public domain.

4. Joshua Bote, "'Get in Good Trouble, Necessary Trouble': Rep. John Lewis in His Own Words," *USA Today*, July 18, 2020, https://www.usatoday.com/story/news/politics/2020/07/18/rep-john-lewis-most-memorable-quotes-get-good-trouble/5464148002.

5. Longfellow, "The Village Blacksmith."

Chapter 10

1. "Obelisk of St. Peter's Square," St. Peter's Basilica, accessed November 6, 2023, https://www.stpetersbasilicatickets.com/obelisk-of-st-peters-square.

2. "Obelisk of St. Peter's Square," St. Peter's Basilica.

3. "Cleopatra's Needle," Ancient Egypt Foundation, accessed November 6, 2023, https://www.ancientegyptfoundation.org/cleopatras_needle.shtml.

CHAPTER 11

1. "World Watch List 2023," Open Doors, https://www.opendoors.org/en-US/persecution/countries.
2. Zach Dawes Jr., "Global Christian Population Projected to Reach 3.3 Billion by 2050," Good Faith Media, February 13, 2023, https://goodfaithmedia.org/global-christian-population-projected-to-reach-3-3-billion-by-2050/#:~:text=Annual%20Christian%20population%20growth%20rates,%25)%20and%20Europe%20(0.04%25).
3. "Jack Is Back in Court, Again. Enough Is Enough," Alliance Defending Freedom, https://adflegal.org/client/jack-phillips.
4. "The Persecution of Jack Phillips Should End," *National Review*, January 30, 2023, https://www.nationalreview.com/2023/01/the-persecution-of-jack-phillips-should-end.
5. Barronelle Stutzman, "Why a Friend Is Suing Me: the Arlene's Flowers Story," *Seattle Times*, November 9, 2015, https://www.seattletimes.com/opinion/why-a-good-friend-is-suing-me-the-arlenes-flowers-story.
6. "Arlene's Flowers v. State of Washington," Alliance Defending Freedom, accessed November 6, 2023, https://adflegal.org/case/arlenes-flowers-v-state-washington.
7. "Florist Who Refused Same-Sex Wedding Job Settles With Washington State Couple," NBC Bay Area, November 18, 2021, https://www.nbcbayarea.com/news/national-international/florist-who-refused-same-sex-wedding-job-settles-washington-state-couple/2736275.
8. Paradise Afshar, "Football Coach Who Won Supreme Court Case for Right to Pray on the Field Resigns After One Game," CNN, September 6, 2023, https://www.cnn.com/2023/09/06/us/washington-football-coach-pray-resigns/index.html.
9. William Wolfe, "Yes, Christians Are Being Persecuted in America. Here's How We Can Respond," *Christian Post*, July 18, 2022, https://www.christianpost.com/voices/yes-christians-are-being-persecuted-in-america.html.
10. "Intercultural and Interreligious Dialogue and Panel Discussion on 'Building Bridges Between East and West,'" United Nations Web TV, June 14, 2023, https://media.un.org/en/asset/k1d/k1dumy7i8b.

CHAPTER 13

1. From *John G. Paton, Missionary to the New Hebrides: An Autobiography* (New York: Fleming H. Revell, 1890), cited in Billy Graham, *Angels: God's Secret Agents* (Garden City, NY: Doubleday, 1975), 2–3.
2. Bible Study Tools, s.v. *"zizanion,"* accessed November 8, 2023, https://www.biblestudytools.com/lexicons/greek/nas/zizanion.html#:~:text=dziz%2Dan'%2Dee%2D,except%20the%20grains%20are%20black.
3. Sarah Laskow, "Wheat's Evil Twin Has Been Intoxicating Humans for Centuries," Atlas Obscura, March 22, 2016, https://www.atlasobscura.com/articles/wheats-evil-twin-has-been-intoxicating-humans-for-centuries.

CHAPTER 14

1. "Great Awakening," *History*, A&E Television Networks, September 20, 2019, https://www.history.com/topics/european-history/great-awakening.

About the Author

P HIL HOTSENPILLER IS the founder and senior pastor of
Influence Church in Anaheim Hills, California, and
president of AmericanFaith.com, a news media outlet.
A dynamic blend of entrepreneur, author, and art aficionado,
he consistently bridges the divide between leadership, artistic
expression, and the pulse of contemporary society.

His voice resonates in the media landscape, with notable interactions spanning outlets such as *The Washington Post*, Fox News,
CNN, The History Channel, and *The Telegraph*. As president of
the New York Executive Coaching Group, Phil empowers CEOs,
presidents, and other industry leaders to surpass their professional and personal benchmarks. His clientele spans Fortune 500
magnates to luminaries in the arts, finance, and philanthropic
sectors.

Academically distinguished, Phil holds a BA and an MDiv.
His pursuit of knowledge led him to postgraduate endeavors at
Oxford University. He is the author of eleven books, including
his highly acclaimed best-selling book *One Nation Without Law*.